HIDDEN HISTORY

of

SOUTH JERSEY

From the Capitol to the Shore

GORDON BOND

Charleston   London

THE
History
PRESS

Published by The History Press
Charleston, SC 29403
www.historypress.net

Cover image courtesy of the Library of Congress.

First published 2013

Manufactured in the United States

ISBN 978.1.62619.009.2

Library of Congress CIP data applied for.

For Onslow and Daisy

CONTENTS

PREFACE

New Jersey has always had something of a split personality, tugged as we are between the cultural weights of two urban centers, New York and Philadelphia. We have to work harder, it seems, to assert that we are more than merely their respective suburbs, though we will be happy to let you pass through from one to the other...so long as you pay the tolls for the privilege, of course.

The dynamics of this bipolar cross-river combination of symbiosis and rivalry have colored our history in some important ways. Quaker influence from the City of Brotherly Love, for example, made South Jersey an abolitionist stronghold and the destination of many fugitive slaves crossing the bay from the slave state of Delaware. By contrast, the relationship between New York's mercantile interests and the Deep South generated a self-serving sympathy for the Confederacy that bled into North Jersey across the Hudson River.

These days, such regional difference manifests itself in such banal things as fealty to respective sports franchises. Yet, broadly speaking, North Jersey remains more industrial, while South Jersey retains its agrarian and maritime flavors—with a vaguely defined buffer of Central Jersey somewhere in between. Occasionally, however, the cultural divide becomes more sharpened. In 1980, for example, a satirical suggestion that South Jersey secede and form its own state took on a serious life of its own. South Jerseyans were upset that the state government was supporting the Meadowlands Complex development in North Jersey while dismissing their own Garden State Race Track plans.

More recently, South Jersey's history communities have lamented what they perceive as a northern bias when celebrating—and, more importantly, funding—state history projects. It's hard to say if this is an intentional snub or a statistical trick of the light (North Jersey is more densely populated, for example).

But one thing is certain: a lot of significant, fascinating and diverse history happened at the Garden State's southern end. Some stories are better known, but this book seeks to focus on some of the lesser-known gems— connections South Jersey has with broader histories, from paleontology to capital punishment, from American car culture to fugitive slaves, from rock-and-roll to tea burning. All serve to remind us of the amazing history to be found in every corner of *our* New Jersey.

Thanks are due to several people who helped to make this book possible. Through some serendipity, Ronald L. Becker, head of Special Collections and University Archives, Rutgers University Libraries, alerted me to the addition of the Carl F. Adams papers to their collection, which inspired the chapter in this book about Adams and his odd twist to the Trenton slogan, "Trenton Makes—the World Takes." Thanks also to author Dennis Rizzo, whose mention of Harriet Tubman's time in Cape May in his book, *Parallel Communities*, inspired me to explore that aspect of her career more closely. My sincere thanks to Stephanie M. Hoagland, my wife, my fellow history geek and my tireless proofreader. Thanks to Whitney Landis for patiently dealing with the issues over the images. And I would be remiss were I not to acknowledge Onslow and Daisy, my feline companions while writing this book.

GORDON BOND
Union, New Jersey
May 2013

Chapter 1

BONE WARS IN THE GARDEN

B ribery, theft, vandalism and slander are not normally acts one would associate with the realm of science—unless, of course, it was a "mad scientist" bent on world domination. Yet each was a feature of perhaps the most famous scientific feud in history. It has gone down by two names. One was "The Great Dinosaur Rush," but perhaps more viscerally accurate was "The Bone Wars." Set against the Gilded Age, it would prove to be a dispute that would ultimately consume and destroy the two protagonists in almost Shakespearean style. For two weeks, it even scandalized the average public, who followed the newspaper stories telling of enormous bones of fantastical ancient beasts with unpronounceable names being unearthed in America's wild and wooly West. It was all as big and gaudy as the excesses of the era, the vastness of the landscape and the egos of the men enjoined.

And it all started in South New Jersey.

Dinosaur Mania

Dinosaurs are cool—bizarre creatures of monstrous proportions right out of our nightmares yet able to be regarded from the safe distance of ancient history. Not that the current record-holding giant would have presented much of a threat—*Argentinosaurus* was a vegetarian. But since some scientists estimate them to have grown from 98 to 110 feet long and to have weighed between 80 and 110 tons, you probably still would have wanted to keep out of their way. Paradoxically, it was one of the smaller varieties—not much bigger than an adult human male—that seems to have been truly nightmarish. The movie *Jurassic Park* made a pop star out of the *Velociraptor*, with its ghastly sickle-like rear claw.

But there are also the "classics" any schoolchild worth his or her skinned knees can name: *Triceratops, Tyrannosaurus Rex, Stegosaurus, Brontosaurus* (which a more precocious child might know is now called *Apatosaurus*) and the *Pterodactyl*. Beyond physical size, diversity and downright strangeness, dinosaurs present tantalizing mysteries. We know them as bones, yet they were once living, breathing, dynamic creatures. What did they really look like? What color were they? Did their flesh sport patterns? Feathers, even? How did they live? Then there is the cautionary tale of how these once-dominant life forms were toppled from their ecological perch—or did some of them evolve into birds?

We humans have been at least peripherally aware of these beasts since farmers or quarry workers first unearthed mysteriously huge bones. With no particular reason to think they were remnants of a long-disappeared species, early cultures interpreted them as proof of their respective mythologies. The Chinese, for example, called them *konglong*, meaning "terrible dragon," and villagers still grind them up as ingredients in traditional medicines—much to the horror of paleontologists. Back in 1677, a British chemistry professor at the University of Oxford, Robert Plot, believed that a bone fragment found

in a Cromwell limestone quarry was from the femur of one of the giant humans of the Bible. Others explained the bone as being from an animal that missed Noah's Ark and perished in the Great Flood. We now know that it was from a dinosaur, *Megalosaurus*.

Portrait of Robert Plot, DD, by Sylvester Harding. Plot believed the dinosaur bone found in a quarry belonged to a race of giants mentioned in the Bible. *British Museum, London.*

The eccentric Reverend William Buckland was the first to describe a complete dinosaur in a scientific journal.

Nevertheless, that the true picture these puzzle pieces were ultimately describing became clear at all is rather remarkable. Fossilization is a rare enough process, meaning even fragmentary specimens—let alone anything close to a complete skeleton—are uncommon. It was fortuitous, then, that there were areas of England conducive to creating and preserving fossils. Between 1815 and 1825, the rather eccentric Reverend William Buckland was able to collect enough fragments to attempt a description of a complete animal in a scientific journal. He was both a theologian and geologist who tried reconciling the seemingly lengthy geologic record with the comparatively brief one described by his Bible. But he has been equally remembered for holding it as a personal goal to eat at least one of every creature in the animal kingdom, a penchant for collecting coprolites (fossilized feces) and conducting fieldwork in his academic gowns. Odd though he may have been, he did describe the first dinosaur, the *Megalosaurus*—the same type from which Plot's femur had come.

While he described the animal based on the bones, the actual term "dinosaur" would have to wait for Sir Richard Owen in 1841. He first coined *Dinosauria*, meaning "Terrible Reptile" or even "Fearfully Great Reptile." Owen was another of paleontology's controversial if brilliantly prolific characters. On the plus side, he was not only a driving force behind London's British Museum of Natural History in 1881 but also argued that it should be accessible to *everyone*, not just academia. Indeed, our modern egalitarian conception of what a museum is can be traced to his philosophies. But he could also apparently be something of a jerk. In a premonition of things to come in the field, he feuded with Gideon Mantell, whose efforts at

Left: Sir Richard Owen was the first to coin the term *Dinosauria* in 1841. He is shown here in in 1856 with the skull of a crocodile. *Albumen print from wet collodion on glass negative, Maull & Polyblank, 1856.*

Right: Gideon Mantell's efforts at reconstructing an *Iguanodon* skeleton mark an early milestone in the development of paleontology. *Dinosaurs: A Concise Natural History.*

reconstructing the skeleton of an *Iguanodon* are considered another founding event in the scientific study of the creatures. Owen intentionally worked to steal credit, falsely claiming the discovery of the fossils belonged to himself and Georges Cuvier. He is said to have taken perverse delight in making sure Mantell's papers were never published, actively attempting to ruin his career. While historians debate how unpleasant Owen really was—or just unfairly maligned by rivals—a once-brilliant career descended into bitter personal and professional acrimony, losing him credibility in the emerging field.

Despite such antics, by the mid-1800s, the scientific discipline of paleontology was becoming established. While most of the key discoveries had been made in Europe, the American landscape was also about to yield some spectacular finds—and launch its own scientific feud.

Bones in the Garden

New Jersey is a small state, ranking forty-seventh out of the fifty, with 7,417 square miles of land. For context, around seventy-seven New Jerseys would fit in the area of the largest state, Alaska. (Yet Alaska's *entire* population equals that of New Jersey's Hudson County alone.) But as with so many other aspects, the Garden State packs a remarkable amount of diversity within its borders—and that includes its geology.

A walk from the northwest corner of the state down through the interior to Cape May would be an effective (and exhausting) walk through geologic time, albeit not always in order. The bedrock of the extreme northwest, for example, is largely Paleozoic slate, limestone and sandstone—between 2,500 and 1,600 million years old. The Highlands south of it, however, are mostly granite from the older Achaean, 3,800 to 2,500 million years old and the oldest rocks in New Jersey. Continuing south is a band of Triassic red sandstone and shale from 251 to 199.6 million years ago.

If you drew a line between the mouth of the Raritan River on the east side and Trenton on the west, the Achaean, Paleozoic and Triassic formations would all be above it, in the upper third of the state. Everything south of that line is sedimentary, reflecting an interesting aspect of New Jersey's geologic history that would play a role in the preservation of fossils.

The evolution of the Garden State's landscape over the millions of years has been shaped to a surprising degree by the glacial cycles. It makes sense, however, when it is remembered that New Jersey can be described as a coastal peninsula. During ice ages, when large quantities of the planet's water were locked away in the glaciers, sea levels dropped, causing more land to be exposed. And, equally, during the periods when the glaciers melted, that freed water caused the sea levels to rise, submerging low-lying lands under shallow seas. Given the lower elevations of the southern two-thirds of the state, much of New Jersey alternated between being above and below water as the shorelines and rivers migrated over time. Sediments from the ocean on one side and rivers on the other were slowly deposited, layer upon layer, over the vast coastal planes covering roughly that bottom two-thirds of the state.

This Coastal Plane is further divided between the "Inner" and "Outer." The Outer Coastal Plane covers everything south of a line running roughly from Long Branch to Salem and is the younger of the two, relatively speaking, dating between 65.0 to 2.6 million years ago. Between this and the Triassic is a strip running from Raritan Bay southwest to where the Delaware River curves around Salem County. This is the Inner Coastal Plain, where deposits date back to the Cretaceous, between around 145.5 and 65.5 million years ago. Both planes abound in sand and clay, but it's the Inner Plane where one finds a hardened freshwater mud that includes calcium carbonate, called "marl." This hardens into "marlstone" and is excellent for the preservation of fossils.

What makes marl so good at preserving fossils is that it is a sedimentary rock. It starts as silt—sands deposited by ocean tides or transported from inland to the sea via rivers and streams. Obviously, the association with water means lots of dead marine organisms, large and small, get added to any given layer. But land animals and plants can also be washed out to sea from floods or by falling directly into a river. Most tend to get devoured by scavengers, decompose or be eroded away. But where the sediment accumulates fast enough, organisms can be buried before they get disturbed by these other agents. Where igneous and metamorphic rocks form at temperatures and pressures that tend to destroy organic materials, sedimentary rocks form at a slow, cool, comparatively gentle pace. The remains of a creature or plant can become suspended in the accumulating layers of material, permitting fossilization the opportunity to take place.

Under the slowly building pressure and heat of subsequent layers of sediment, the organic material will still be destroyed, but not before leaving an impression in the hardening stone. Soft tissue, as might be expected, tends to fare worse than bone. But sometimes, if the conditions are just right, as the soft tissue dissolves, water carries minerals into the cavity left behind, where they harden into a cast of what had been there. Known as "permineralization," occasionally even fine, microscopic cellular structures are replicated in stone.

This is, necessarily, a rather simplified explanation, and as might be suspected, the exact conditions for high-fidelity permineralization tend to be rare. But over millions of years of formation, marl offers pretty good odds. Carbonates—like the marl's calcium carbonate—are efficient at it and are the most common permineralization materials (or "cements").

New Jersey's "marl belt" would also prove important in maintaining the Garden State's agriculture identity. The calcium carbonate is excellent for neutralizing acidic soil, and marl became a vital ingredient for fertilizers. While settlers were aware of the rich marl deposits, early farmers found New Jersey's soil already fertile enough without needing such additional fertilizers. By the 1830s, however, they saw the productivity of their land diminish and looked to the marl pits for help, eventually launching a new industry in the mid- to late 1800s. As workmen quarried the marl, they began uncovering fossils—and attracting the attention of the burgeoning field of paleontology, particularly from institutions in nearby Philadelphia.

Not that New Jersey cornered the market on them, by any means. As promising as marl is, fossilization is still a very rare occurrence—and all the more so for large dinosaurs. A small fish or a plant leaf is more likely to get quickly covered up before scavengers or decomposition claim it. By contrast, the numbers of larger dinosaurs that would die near water or get washed into the sea by floods would be small. Additionally, a large carcass takes longer to cover, leaving it vulnerable to destruction before any hope of fossilization can happen. As of 1993, there were only six accepted species of dinosaur considered to have been native to New Jersey—and considering everything working against preservation, it's probably surprising it is even that many. The true number was most likely higher, and bone fragments do hint at as-yet-unidentified species. Marine life is far better represented from those days during the Cretaceous, when northeast North America was separated from the West Coast by a shallow sea and the Inner Coastal Plain was the Jersey Shore. While there's no evidence they roamed New Jersey specifically, this was also the era of such perennial favorites as *Triceratops* and the equally popular *Tyrannosaurus*.

Nevertheless, South Jersey's marl yielded up a dinosaur all our own.

Hadrosaurus Foulkii

Before 1838, Cooper's Creek's minor claim to anything approaching historically noteworthy fame had been as the location where a boat along the Delaware River sheltered for a night in 1723—among the passengers who camped on the banks was a young runaway apprentice named Benjamin Franklin on his way to Philadelphia.

That changed (somewhat) in 1838, when a local Haddonfield farmer by the name of John Estaugh Hopkins decided to take advantage of the marl buried on a piece of his land along a small tributary that emptied into Cooper's Creek. Digging a pit, he uncovered some large bones and brought them home as curiosities, even putting them on display in his house for the next twenty years. In 1858, William Parker Foulke, a lawyer with a penchant for paleontology over in Philadelphia, caught wind of the farmer's display.

Born in Philadelphia in 1816, Foulke studied law and had argued cases before the Pennsylvania Supreme Court. His scientific avocations—where his heart really seemed to lie—earned him election to a membership in the American Philosophical Society on October 20, 1854. He had been a member of the Academy of Natural Science since 1849 and the Historical Society of Pennsylvania since 1842.

His interests were rather varied. He would also help in finding backing for the arctic explorer Isaac I. Hayes's expedition to the North Pole in 1860–61. But they also extended to the controversial social issues of his day. In 1845, he had become a manager of the Pennsylvania Colonization Society, the state's branch of the Society for the Colonization of Free People of Color of America. Founded the year Foulke had been born, the society supported abolition but didn't see much hope for freed blacks in white America. Its answer, well meant if misguided, was to send them all back to Africa—notwithstanding that by that point most slaves had been born in the United States. Toward that end, it had worked to establish the colony of Liberia. Foulke and others had thought the coastal location unhealthy and lobbied for settlement in the hill country farther inland. An appropriations bill in Congress for their site, however, lost by a single vote.

Prison reform was another area of interest. In 1845, he joined the Philadelphia Society for Alleviating the Miseries of Public Prisons, making a study of methods of discipline that he used to influence the designs of his friend, the architect John Haviland, when designing Pennsylvania's then-groundbreaking Eastern State Penitentiary. His name would be attached to several of the state's reform bills—indeed, as many pages of his 1868 obituary, published in the *Proceedings of the American Philosophical Society*, were devoted to that subject as were to his dinosaur work.

In 1858, Foulke later told the *Proceedings of the Academy of Natural Sciences of Philadelphia*, he had spent the summer and fall at Haddonfield, where his neighbor was none other than John E. Hopkins. The farmer told Foulke of the large bones he had dug from his marl pit twenty years before—bones that sounded to Foulke like vertebrae. Unfortunately, Hopkins related, he was still young when he found them and not aware of their value, so when people expressed interest in them after seeing them at his house, he gave them away—and he couldn't recall who had been the recipients of the curious souvenirs. Nevertheless, this gave Foulke an idea. Hopkins only remembered the backbones and maybe a shoulder blade. Maybe if he dug around the area some more, other bones might yet be found.

Hopkins gave Foulke *carte blanche* to dig wherever he wanted and take whatever he found. The problem was, he had a hard time remembering the exact spot where he had found the bones—the pit had long since been filled back in to the common ground level and overgrown. Nevertheless, between the memories of Hopkins and the workmen who had been employed at the time of discovery, they found the original pit.

Somewhere between nine and ten feet down, workmen hit a cache of bones. Freeing them from the marl would be painstaking, but Foulke called in some experts who concluded that it would be well worth the effort. The importance of the bones they uncovered would have to wait for subsequent interpretation.

Stories also emerged from other marl pits of bones having been discarded by workmen unaware of their significance. A blacksmith identified only as "Mr. King" had a collection of bones but had given most away. All, that is, but for three jaw fragments from a *Mosasaurus*—an aquatic, carnivorous lizard, sometimes described as a flippered crocodile. These stories of treasures lost—and so close to the centers of learning at Philadelphia to boot—served as cautionary tales, alerting paleontologists and geologists of the potential beneath South Jersey's marl belt. Alliances would need to be cultivated with marl pit landowners and workers alike.

Fortunately, however, at least one unnamed workman from Hopkin's farm had his interest piqued. Working in another pit near the White Horse Tavern, some six miles south of Haddonfield, he had the presence of mind to alert Foulke of vertebrae, teeth and long bones he found—the remains of an ancient crocodile not before known to have been in New Jersey.

Among the experts Foulke had called on was Joseph Leidy, a professor of anatomy at the University of Pennsylvania. While paleontology was an accepted discipline, it was still the province of generally well-off and enthusiastic amateurs. Leidy made his living as a professor of a longer-established field but, like Foulke, had a range of other interests of which the bones of ancient creatures was but one. Where Foulke was also involved with social issues, however, Leidy's activities were more confined to the sciences—though perhaps no less socially influential. In 1846, for example, he was among the first to work out that the illness of trichinosis was caused by a parasite in undercooked meat. It was also the same year he became the first person to have solved a murder mystery using a microscope. Like a nineteenth-century version of *CSI*, he determined that the blood on the clothing and axe of a man accused of killing a Philadelphia farmer was *not* that of chickens he claimed to have been slaughtering but from a human source. The suspect later confessed.

Leidy's career with bones—reflected in some 553 papers, articles and books—would include identifying many now-extinct species of both

In addition to paleontology, Joseph Leidy contributed to the early application of science to solving crimes.

dinosaurs and early mammals not before known to have lived in North America. But he would become best known for what he made out of Foulke's Haddonfield find. In December 1858, Leidy was able to stand before the Academy of Natural Sciences in Philadelphia and declare that the twenty-eight vertebrae, a humerus (upper arm bone), a complete radius and ulna (the two lower arm bones), an ilium and pubis bone (from the pelvis), a femur (thigh bone), a tibia (shin bone), a fibula (calf bone), two metatarsals (foot bones), a first phalanx (toe bone), nine teeth and a piece of a lower jaw were enough for him to say that this was a new genus of dinosaur, never before seen. It resembled the *Iguanodon* of Europe but was different enough to be unique. As the first to identify it, the honor of naming it fell to him— the *Hadrosaurus foulkii*, paying homage to both the New Jersey town and the man who found it.

A feature that struck Leidy was how the humerus was twenty inches long, while the femur was forty inches—a disparity that at first led him to wonder if they were not from different animals. This disproportion between the fore and hind legs suggested a then-unusual conclusion. It was presumed that dinosaurs walked on all fours (other clearly bipedal dinosaurs, like *Tyrannosaurus*, were yet to be discovered). But the configuration of *Hadrosaurus* seemed to indicate the animal walked on its hind legs, perhaps supporting itself with its tail. Its teeth showed it to have been an herbivore, so a stance that put the mouth near the ground made sense had it been a grazer. Leidy hedged his bet a little, but

William Parker Foulke is credited with first identifying *Hadrosaurus*, New Jersey's state dinosaur. *American Philosophical Society.*

he is now credited as one of the first to recognize that some dinosaurs did indeed walk on two legs instead of four.

Given the vagrancies of the fossilization process, "complete" is a relative term when it comes to dinosaur skeletons. Those mounted in museums comprise a percentage of "real" fossils and fabrications based on logical assumptions of the rest. By 1858, only finds from Europe had enough surviving bones to be credibly identified. In America, it had mostly been fragments, isolated bones or a handful of teeth—not enough to say with certainty what the rest of the animal looked like. But all that changed with *Hadrosaurus foulkii*—this was the first time enough bones were found to permit identification.

In 1868, *Hadrosaurus foulkii* also became the first skeleton to be mounted, along with castings of educated guesses of what the missing bones looked like. Englishman Benjamin Waterhouse Hawkins was given the task, drawing from his experience as a sculptor and natural history illustrator. Working with Leidy, he determined that the correct stance was upright, firmly on the back two legs and using the tail for support. Since then, subsequent bipedal dinosaur specimens appear to indicate a more horizontal stance—with the backbone more parallel to the ground. The hind legs still support the weight and provide locomotion, but the tail is held aloft, off the ground behind, as a counterweight, freeing up the forearms.

In 1991, *Hadrosaurus* was appointed New Jersey's official "state dinosaur." But the find had put South Jersey on the proverbial paleontological radar right from the start.

Edward Cope

A young family arrived at Haddonfield in 1867, led by a thirty-year-old man with hair parted like an open book and sporting what we today might consider a Colonel Sanders–style mustache and goatee combo. Edward Drinker Cope was taking a calculated risk in coming to South Jersey, lured by the bones in the marl pits.

Born on July 28, 1840, to well-off Philadelphia Quakers, Cope had always exhibited a penchant for science, even as a child. These interests would be both encouraged and discouraged by his father, Alfred. (Cope's mother, Hanna, died when he was three; his father remarried Rebecca Biddle.) The family went on trips throughout New England, visiting museums, zoos and gardens, and young Edward explored the exotic gardens of their eight-acre Fairfield estate, showing a talent for drawing and painting nature. Alfred used his own upbringing as the model for his son's education—at age nine, Edward was sent to a day school, and at twelve, he was packed off to the Friend's Boarding School near West Chester, Pennsylvania. There, he learned algebra, chemistry, scripture, physiology, grammar, astronomy, Latin—and that he could get money out of his father. It already cost Alfred $500 a year in tuition—not a small sum in the 1850s. But letters home expressing loneliness and requesting a larger allowance were met with acquiescence in a pattern that would be repeated even when Edward was an adult. Indeed, some historians characterize him as having been something of a spoiled brat. He could also be argumentative with infamous flares of temper he never grew out of.

He didn't always do well in school, and his penmanship would always leave much to be desired. But what enthusiasm he lacked for subjects he didn't like, he made up for with one that he did: biology. Not only did he make frequent trips to Philadelphia's Academy of Natural Sciences on his own, but he also pored over natural history books in his spare time. It seems he was something of a nerd—and proud of it.

But Edward would end up caught between his own desires and the direction his father thought his life should take. Alfred made sure Edward was sent to the farm during his summer breaks in 1854 and 1855. After the spring of 1856, he didn't return to school at all. Instead, Alfred bought his son farmland. Science might be a gentlemanly enough hobby, but farming was a sober and noble way a grown man could earn a good living.

His father may have intended the best, but farming simply held no appeal for Edward. He wanted to be a scientist. Even while working on the farm, he used his free time to study on his own. He convinced the skeptical, if pliable, Alfred to pay for private tutoring, learning French and German. And he found something of a compromise—he would rent out the land and use the proceeds to finance his intellectual pursuits.

If nothing else, young Cope was driven and persistent. In 1861, his father at last relented and agreed to pay his son's way at the University of Pennsylvania. There, he studied under none other than Joseph Leidy, perhaps hearing firsthand of his *Hadrosaurus* successes. At Leidy's urging, his student joined the Academy of Natural Sciences, finding a job re-cataloguing its herpetological collection.

He was able to lay claim to something of an identity as a scientist thanks to the publishing outlet provided by membership with the Academy of Natural Sciences and American Philosophical Society. In 1861, at age twenty-one, he was first published—a paper about *Salamandidae* classification—and he began specializing in reptiles and amphibians.

What he didn't have yet was a degree.

What got in the way was the outbreak of the Civil War. While many men his age ran off to seek battlefield glory, that idea clashed with his Quaker pacifist sensibilities—but also his intellectual ambitions. Nevertheless, perhaps caught up in the national fervor for service and sacrifice, he entertained notions of possibly working to help transition former slaves into freedom (his father had been an abolitionist) or maybe serve in a Union field hospital. Here, Leidy's experience may have again shaped Cope's choices. Leidy had volunteered for a field hospital, and his descriptions of the horrors he witnessed might have been what pushed the idea from Cope's mind.

Rather than deal with the crisis at home, he would wait out the conflict on the fashionable "Grand Tour" of Europe. He secured meetings with some of the most distinguished scientists of the day throughout France, Germany, Great Britain, Ireland, Austria, Italy and Eastern Europe. Yet his letters home have the feel of someone intellectually adrift.

In the winter of 1863, Cope was in Berlin, where he first encountered his eventual nemesis, Othniel Charles Marsh. In many ways, they were already opposites. Where Cope came from a well-to-do family, Marsh's upbringing in Lockport, New York, was more modest. Indeed, it might have remained so had his intellectual ambitions not been facilitated by the good fortune of having the wealthy George Peabody for an

Edward Drinker Cope.

uncle. With Peabody's support, Marsh was able to study at Yale, graduating in 1860, and also take the "Grand Tour," studying anatomy, mineralogy and geology in Europe. It so happened that he was studying at the University of Berlin when Cope was in town. Marsh was older—thirty-two at the time—and had two university degrees. The twenty-three-year-old Cope had none—indeed, he had no formal education beyond age sixteen. But where Marsh had been published but twice, Cope already had thirty-seven published scientific works to his name—as the saying goes, publish or perish.

Yet their differences also seemed to make them complementary, and they got along great. Marsh gave his new friend a tour of the city, and they spent days together, indulging their mutual passions for science. When Cope returned to Philadelphia in 1864, he and Marsh kept in touch via letters and exchanged manuscripts, photographs and fossils. It seemed the start of a fruitful scientific and personal relationship. They even named new species they identified after each other.

If Cope was to be taken seriously for a "real" scientist, he would have to earn a living from it. Here his father would again prove to be his best benefactor, despite his misgivings. Alfred Cope had donated a lot of money to the Quaker-run Haverford College and had influence. He managed to pull some strings and Haverford granted his son an honorary master's

Othniel Charles Marsh.

degree so he could qualify for a professorship job there. While it certainly says something about the influence of money, it is also testimony to Edward Cope's intellectual skill that it would take the chance.

At last settled in a career, he married his cousin, Annie Pim, and a daughter, Julia, was born on June 10, 1866. He still owned the farmland he rented to others as added income for his new family. But his ambitions were too strong. Almost immediately, he was off traveling the American West, sending home descriptions of the animals in letters intended for Julia's education.

He found some pleasure teaching at Haverford but was still driven by a deep need to go his own way and do his own work—and the hours spent at the front of a classroom, while it paid the bills, got in the way of his intellectual fulfillment. South Jersey's marl pits beckoned. Now that diggers knew they were more than odd debris to be thrown away, they began turning up all kinds of tantalizing fossils. Cope wanted to be at the center of that universe.

Aside from being a pleasant village in marl country, Haddonfield had been established in 1701 as a Quaker colony—five hundred acres purchased by John Haddon and settled by his daughter, Elizabeth. Given that influence, it is not surprising that Cope would have friends and family there. And he had also begun to cultivate his contacts among the marl quarrymen, asking that they save any odd bones for him. Periodically, he traveled from Philadelphia to swing by each pit, collecting specimens of ancient turtles, crocodiles, *Mosasaurs* (semi aquatic carnivores) and even a femur from a *Hadrosaur*. To finance his plans, he manipulated more money out of Alfred and cut his ties with the land by having his father sell off the farmland and send him the proceeds.

When the Copes arrived in 1868, they did so in style. In addition to his wife, Anna, and daughter, Julia, was a Negro servant, Esther Ann Still. They moved into 242 King's Highway, a Gothic-style mansion sporting its own water system, windmill, servants' quarters and a barn. It was said to be the finest house in town. Here they would stay for the next eight years—the most productive of Cope's career.

And where the end would begin.

Cope Claims Haddonfield

Alfred Voorhees, owner of the West Jersey Marl Company, had a surprise for Cope. It was 1866—two years before the family settled in Haddonfield—and may have been what cinched the decision to make the move. The workmen at the Barnsboro pit, about a dozen miles southwest of town, had uncovered a massive claw, bits of foot and leg bones and a lower jaw fragment sporting some nasty serrated teeth. No doubt this was a carnivore—and a scary one at that. Cope deduced that it represented a Late Cretaceous relative of the *Megalosaurus* found in England and the *Deinodon* being dug from the American West. In August 1866, he had described it for the Academy of Natural Science as a likely vigorous hunter, given that claw. He named it *Laelaps*, meaning "eagle-clawed leaper." This was a departure from how most paleontologists at the time pictured dinosaurs, as sluggish, dimwitted beasts.

The news piqued the curiosity of Othniel Marsh, with whom Cope had maintained a friendly contact since Berlin. Life had been good to Marsh on his return to the United States in 1866—or, more accurately, his uncle George Peabody had been good to him. The seventy-one-year-old philanthropist saw his time was limited and, wanting to build his legacy, sought educational institutions upon which to bestow some of his wealth. His nephew convinced him to make a donation of $150,000 to his alma mater of Yale, to establish a new natural history museum. It would be called the Peabody Museum of Natural History, and Marsh would curate it. Up to then, Yale's collections were primarily of the mineral type. Marsh wanted to expand it to include fossils, establishing both the Peabody as a premier institution of learning and himself as the premier paleontologist.

While fossils were being found out West, expeditions into the then still wilderness were difficult and costly. Perfectly respectable specimens could be dug from the East Coast, not all that far from New Haven, Connecticut, down in New Jersey. So Marsh wrote to Cope asking if he would be so kind as to give him a tour of the famous marl pits.

As Cope and Marsh drove their horse-drawn carriage from marl pit to marl pit, it might have dawned on Marsh that friend Cope stood in his way.

An early representation of *Laelaps* as it was thought to have carried itself in life. *E.D. Cope, "The Fossil Reptiles of New Jersey," American Naturalist 3 (1869): 84–91.*

Both men had dinosaur-sized egos and ambitions to match. Cope saw South Jersey as his turf—it was as if he were still a gentleman farmer, but instead of crops being plucked from the soil, it was dinosaur fossils. Marsh paid attention, not just to the locations and what was being produced, but also to who the players were in the industry. Somewhere along the way, he concocted a scheme. Behind Cope's back, he would bribe the marl pit men to send their fossils not across the Delaware to Cope's Philadelphia institutions but up to Connecticut, to Marsh's Peabody Museum. The pit owner who would prove most willing to go along with Marsh's scheme? Alfred Voorhees.

Marsh's underhanded tactic is, of course, ethically questionable. But so too was Cope's presumption that he could "claim" South Jersey as his own personal fossil-hunting grounds. Not long after, Cope found himself shut out of the marl pits, which were now open to Marsh.

The war had begun.

Wrong End Foremost

Some Bone War historians have come to gloss over the provocations in the marl pits, preferring instead to focus on a more melodramatic moment that had its origins out on the west Kansas frontiers.

On June 22, 1867, the forty-man garrison at Fort Wallace defended itself against an attack by a reported four hundred Native Americans. When it was done, eight soldiers were killed or would die of their wounds, along with an estimated twenty of their attackers. The assault on the fort was likely by either the Cheyenne or Sioux, who periodically harassed white settlers and workers on what was then the westernmost terminus of the Union Pacific Railroad. The fort had been established to provide some defense.

That any sort of science would come from the area may be surprising, but the U.S. Army surgeon who would have treated the men's wounds, Dr. Theophilus H. Turner, had made an important discovery. At least he knew the significance when he saw some big bones emerging from an eroded ravine some fourteen miles north of the fort. Pulling three massive vertebrae from what he later described as the "skeleton of an extinct monster," he gave two to John LeConte, a naturalist who was part of the railroad's surveying teams. When LeConte was done with the job that November, he showed the bones to Edward Cope back in Philadelphia. Cope was excited, immediately recognizing them as having likely come from a *Plesiosaur*—a long-necked aquatic carnivore of the late Cretaceous. So, on December 3, 1867, he wrote directly to Turner, offering that if he could dig out the rest, the Academy of Natural Sciences would pick up the tab to have them shipped to Philadelphia. Procuring extra muscle from the men at the fort, by February 1868, he was able to tell Cope he had recovered "something over thirty-five feet of its vertebrae" and that "there is a large amount of bony matter contained in a very hard stone matrix, some of which retains its connection with the backbone."

Turner planned on waiting for the completion of the railroad to ship, expected in late 1868, but an eager Cope managed to convince him to arrange for an army wagon train to carry them in late February the ninety miles to where a train east could be found. Half a month and some 1,500 miles later, Cope opened the crates. It has been suggested by some historians, however, that he may have been *too* excited to get his hands on the bones.

As mentioned, skeletons are normally not complete, so a degree of educated guesswork goes into imagining what the complete animal might have looked like. Cope's background was as a herpetologist—someone who studies lizards. And lizards tend to have short necks and long tails. So to him it made sense to arrange the extant vertebrae in a manner that would put the head on the assumed short end of the spine.

Cope issued his description to the academy on March 24, 1868, calling it "an animal related to the *Plesiosaurus*," which he called *Elasmosaurus platyurus*. He had the bones assembled for display at its museum, and leading scientists had been invited to view it, including Marsh. Cope was likely still smarting from Marsh's still-fresh subterfuge but apparently showed off his find to him nonetheless, perhaps seeing it as an opportunity to rub his success in his rival's face.

What happened next is subject to debate. One version has Marsh pointing out, loudly, how Cope had, in fact, put the head on the wrong end. Known

Plesiosaur skeletons suggested very long necks—the opposite of the lizards Cope was used to. Some cite this alleged public humiliation before his peers as the moment Cope's war with Marsh began in earnest. Among those to accept this version is Jane Pierce Davidson, in her 1997 book *The Bone Sharp: The Life of Edward Drinker Cope*, issued by the Academy of Natural Sciences of Philadelphia to mark the centennial of his death.

Others, however, question Marsh's role in how the mistake was revealed. Some twenty years after the fact, in 1890, Marsh described the moment for the *New York Herald*:

> *The skeleton itself was arranged in the Museum of the Philadelphia Academy of Sciences, according to this restoration, and when Professor Cope showed it to me and explained its peculiarities, I noticed that the articulations of the vertebrae were reversed and suggested to him gently that he had the whole thing wrong end foremost. His indignation was great, and he asserted in strong language that he had studied the animal for many months and ought to at least know one end from the other.*

By then, the war between them was raging, so it would have been in Marsh's interest to bury what he had done in South Jersey, focusing instead on Cope's "indignation" over a "gentle" suggestion. Some point to Marsh's not having had much experience with *Plesiosaur* skeletons to question if he even noticed the error, let alone pointed it out to Cope's public embarrassment.

The irony is that the man who really did (at least demonstrably) bring Cope's mistake to light in the science world was Joseph Leidy, whose own 1870 description and interpretation of the bones included the line, "Prof. Cope has described the skeleton in a reversed position to the true one."

The Wikipedia.com entry for *Elasmosaurus* claims firmly that no documentary evidence supports Marsh's complicity in embarrassing Cope.

Beyond this, paleontological claim jumping and competition to be the first to describe a new creature would become the main thrust and parry of their growing intellectual duel. Another South Jersey–related example of how such often questionable—if not downright underhanded—means were employed has also been cited as the spark that lit the fuse.

When a clergyman, Dr. Samuel Lockwood, found some massive bones on the shore of Union Beach on the Raritan Bay in Monmouth County in 1869, he immediately thought of Othniel Marsh. He wrote to him up at Yale's Peabody Museum in New Haven. Marsh wrote back that he wanted to examine them himself and would shortly come down to visit Lockwood.

How Cope came to learn of the bones is unclear, but he evidently showed up on the clergyman's doorstep, insistent that he be allowed to see them. Confused, Lockwood at first demurred but then relented. Cope stayed just long enough to take measurements, make some sketches and take notes.

And to beat Marsh in publishing a description. William B. Ghallagher asserts this act as the beginning of the dispute proper in his 1997 book, *When Dinosaurs Roamed New Jersey*.

Later, Marsh bought the same specimen from Lockwood for his museum. It must have galled him that while he had the physical prize, the name plaque identified it by Cope's designation of *Ornithotarsus humanis*. It had come from what was evidently an unusually large *Hadrosaur*.

If the name indeed bothered him, Marsh would have a chance to get back at Cope. As described before, among the treasures pulled from Alfred Voorhees's marl pit had been bones of a carnivore Cope had named *Laelaps aquilunguis*. In 1877, Marsh noted that the name *Laelaps* had already been assigned to a species of spider before Cope used it. By convention, to avoid any confusion, the two could not have the same name, and since its arachnid use predated Cope's, it was the dinosaur that would need to be renamed. Marsh likely took pleasure in being the one to correct Cope's oversight—maybe for the second time? While not an unapt choice, Marsh's selection of *Dryptosaurus*, or "wounding reptile," could be seen as having a double meaning.

The Great Dinosaur Rush

In the 1870s, paleontology shifted its focus to the vast planes of the American West and the truly big bones it was yielding. The Cope/Marsh feud followed, expanding as if to take advantage of the extra room, growing to the full bluster that would almost outdo the genuine science it produced.

The first half of the decade saw Cope attaching himself to the U.S. Geological Survey in an unpaid capacity. It was an excuse to get his trowel into the Eocene bone beds of Wyoming. The problem was that the expedition leader, Dr. Ferdinand Vandeveer Hayden, had been letting another prospect for fossils in the same area—none other than Cope's old professor, Joseph Leidy. It seems both men were under the impression they were owed exclusive access, and overlap soon led to a side feud between Cope and Leidy.

Marsh had been under his own impression that he was owed loyalty by the men he hired to prospect and dig fossils for his Peabody Museum. In reality, they went with whoever paid them, leading to Cope unknowingly hiring two of Marsh's men and Marsh's men accidentally shipping finds to Cope. The year 1873 saw the start of a true "Great Dinosaur Rush" between Cope, Marsh and Leidy. Specimens were pulled from the ground and telegrams dashed back east staking claims on new species. There would be time enough later to examine the bones more closely and write up formal papers. True to the old saying, the haste of trumping rivals did indeed make waste. Cope seems to have been the most rushed, as none of the names he gave his finds would actually stick after more careful examination by others. Marsh took delight in yet again "correcting" Cope, much to his rival's chagrin. Indeed, Cope even tried suggesting an alternate classification system to discredit Marsh.

By the mid-1870s, Cope and Marsh ran out of money and had to go back to their respective corners in Philadelphia and New Haven. They sifted through the backlog of fossils from their respective expeditions, continuing to try and one-up each other.

Not that these two driven, ambitious and egotistical men could stay away for long—not when other western territories were turning up more fossils. They would adopt two different strategies—Cope went out personally, attaching himself to the U.S. Army Corps of Engineers (paid this time), while Marsh stayed in Connecticut, cultivating a network of contacts and workmen from afar. When a Colorado schoolteacher named Arthur Lakes and some friends found some big bones while hiking hear Morrison, Wyoming, he sent a shipment of samples to Marsh. To secure Lakes's secrecy and loyalty—and more specimens—Marsh sent him $100. The trouble was, Lakes had already also sent samples to Cope. Money talked, however, and he had to inform the angry Cope that the prizes would go to Marsh.

Cope wasn't out of the running, though. Naturalist O.W. Lucas sent him samples of fossils he came across in Colorado from an herbivore that was the largest dinosaur then known—certainly bigger than anything Lakes had sent Marsh. Marsh tried to pay off Lucas to come work for him, but he remained loyal to Cope. Marsh was no doubt disturbed by word from contacts with the Union Pacific Railroad that Cope's men were also poking around an area of Como Bluff, Wyoming, where two railroad men had seen huge bones. Marsh quickly secured the two workmen's services, including a contract promising payment and bonuses. The men agreed but were not entirely happy with the terms, causing some resentment. Nevertheless, Marsh had secured Como Bluff and would be the first to describe the now popularly known *Stegosaurus*, *Allosaurus* and *Apatosaurus*.

The resentment over the contract would come back to bite Marsh. The two men leaked rumors of the richness of the bone beds, bringing Cope's men sniffing around. Dissatisfied with the deal with Marsh, one of the men, named Carlin but using the pseudonym of Harlow, started working for Cope, sending fossils from Marsh's turf to Philadelphia.

For the next fifteen years, Cope and Marsh burned through their personal fortunes to fund expeditions. The fierceness of their competition had two effects on the men they employed in their respective quarries. Some would quit in disgust (Lakes, for example, quit Marsh in 1880, returning to his classroom). Others would become sucked in by the competitive spirit, spying on one another's camps, trying to bribe men away, stealing fossils and even destroying specimens rather than risking them being claimed by the other side. On at least one occasion, rival teams took to the childish, if potentially dangerous, tactic of throwing rocks at one another.

Like the generals of armies doing battle on distant fields, Cope and Marsh directed things from the East Coast. Both tried to tear down the professional reputations of the other. Cope's pattern of rushing into print his prolific output gave Marsh plenty of mistakes to use against him. But with no small irony, Marsh was found to have put the wrong skull on an *Apatosaurus* skeleton and claimed it to be a new genus, the *Brontosaurus*.

The occasional newspaper accounts of giant bones being unearthed out west did little to convey the acrimony between Cope and Marsh. Much of the science that was so important to the two men and their professional communities was just so much egghead gibberish to most people. When the *New York Herald* covered the August 1870 meeting of the Association for the Advancement of Science in Troy, New York, it mentioned Cope's contribution: "On the Homologies of the Cranial Bones of the Primary Types of Reptiles." "[T]hough no doubt learned in his investigations," it yawned, "[Cope] partook too much of technicality and tedious details to be interesting to the general listener."

The last phases of the war, however, would be played out on a more public stage.

Bitter War

As much as they tried to hurt each other, Cope and Marsh were in some ways their own worst enemies. Cope might blame Marsh's influence over leaders in institutions of higher learning for his inability to find paying work—which wasn't inaccurate, costing him prospects at the Smithsonian Institution and American Museum of Natural History—but it was also the result of his own well-known prickly temperament.

Marsh was doing better. He had enough political connections that the head of the U.S. Geological Survey, John Wesley Powell, named him its chief paleontologist. Aside from a salary, the position brought him prestige and a revenue stream for his work. His ego, however, and a need to control information, would be his downfall. Former collaborators became enemies over his jealous guarding of conclusions—conclusions they helped to make possible. Workers became embittered toward him over his cavalier approach to paying them. All of which Cope would threaten him over in 1884. Congress was looking to reorganize the U.S. Geological Survey and other overlapping survey and study programs, bringing Marsh's stewardship of the survey under scrutiny. Working with the Princeton University professor of anatomy, Henry Fairfield Osborn, Cope located disgruntled survey workers willing to criticize both Powell and Marsh.

Marsh and Powell successfully defended themselves, but Marsh was mad. He claimed that because Cope had collected his fossils on expeditions paid for by the government, *it* owned them. And it wanted them. This was Marsh's biggest miscalculation. Aside from including in the demand specimens from expeditions paid for out of Cope's own pocket, he might as well have demanded his children. By 1887, his fossil collection was all he had left. He was separated from his wife and daughter, living in a tiny Philadelphia apartment. Back in 1877, he had bought the *American Naturalist*, a journal established in 1867. While a respected peer-reviewed publication today, times were leaner at first, providing no real income. Investment in New Mexico gold mines had failed.

He had nothing left. Nothing but his bones collected over twenty years.

Cope had, however, a secret weapon sitting at the bottom of his desk drawer. All during Marsh's tenure with the survey, he had been keeping an elaborate journal of every error of judgment, every impropriety and every nefarious, underhanded deal. He turned it over to a freelance reporter with the *New York Herald*, William Hosea Ballou, who began publishing the accusations on January 12, 1890. Over the next two weeks, the dirty laundry that had before been kept in the paleontology world's family had been dragged out for the world to see, under the sensational but accurate headline, "Scientists Wage Bitter Warfare." The accusations flew, with Marsh and Powell said to have been guilty of plagiarism, of being corrupt and incompetent and even misappropriating government funds. Congress was paying attention. While they didn't hold hearings on the misappropriation charges, they gave into public sentiment against the perceived waste of money, slashing the survey's budget. Powell asked for Marsh's resignation, which he received, and the Paleontology Department was eliminated. But Cope likely saw his true vindication when the Smithsonian Institution laid claim to a large portion of Marsh's fossil collection, which had, in fact, been collected using government funds.

Things began to look up for Cope. The previous year, he had succeeded Leidy, who died in 1887, as professor of zoology with the University of Pennsylvania. The money wasn't much, but it allowed Anna, Julia and him to move together back into one of the town houses out of which hard times had forced them. He had his family and his fossils and managed to fatally

wound his rival's career. He was writing again, averaging forty-three articles a year and two books. In 1894, he made another prospecting trip out west to South Dakota, Texas and Oklahoma, paid for by the Texas Geological Survey. His daughter, Julia, was married the same year to William H. Collins, a Haverford astronomy professor.

Cope's Pine Street home in Philadelphia as it appears today.

All was not golden, however, in Cope's personal life. Financial hardship and months apart had strained his marriage. When Julia and her new husband moved to Haverford, her mother went with them. Publicly, he cited the long commute to his job and lecture commitments. Privately, he admitted that he and Annie had separated. Rumors persisted that he had had affairs while out west.

Cope began rebuilding his life by selling off his prized fossil collections, often for well under his asking prices. Never completely healthy, Cope became ill and died in 1897 at only fifty-six. Some suggested he succumbed to syphilis, contracted during an extramarital dalliance. A 1995 examination of his skeleton (he had left his body to science) found no evidence, however, and the exact cause remains unknown.

Marsh didn't last much longer, dying of pneumonia at age sixty-six in 1899. His bank account was said to have contained $186.

As much as the rivalry had cost him, Cope was almost addicted to the competition right to the bitter end. When his body was donated to the University of Pennsylvania, it was said it came with one final challenge to Marsh. He wanted his brain measured and compared with Marsh's—brain size being then assumed an indicator of intelligence. Who won that bet will never be known. Marsh elected to take his brain with him to the grave.

Final Accounting

In any such contest, it is natural, if simplistic, to regard it in such terms of winners and losers. Historians do indeed sometimes crown a winner, though who is dependent on criteria. The most common metric is the numbers of new species discovered. Here, Marsh "wins" handily, identifying eighty to Cope's fifty-six, though he did have the advantage of better funding toward the end. Cope outpaced Marsh in terms of the number of publications (1,400 plus) and did manage to fatally wound Marsh's reputation at the end. But the competition came at so great a personal and professional cost to both men that it's almost silly to look at it from that perspective.

In the broader sense, the science of paleontology as a whole was both advanced and retarded by the feud. Before it began, there were just nine known species of dinosaur. Thanks to the Great Dinosaur Rush, a combined 136 new species were added. The excitement generated public interest in the ancient beasts with the unpronounceable names being found on their frontier. Marsh's notice that some dinosaurs resembled birds has been vindicated, and Como Bluff would remain among the richest American bone beds worked.

But while it would survive, the Marsh scandal was a black eye for the U.S. Geological Survey. It made a lot of paleontologists wince as their names were dragged before the public, associated with so sordid and undignified an affair. Stories of rushed digs and dynamiting pits—much of it exaggerated—persisted, causing European paleontologists to view their American colleagues as something of a joke for years after.

Historians tend to focus on the fevered pitch reached at the height of the drama. Yet it all began with two ambitious, egotistical men in a horse-drawn cart touring the marl pits of South Jersey.

Chapter 2

BIRTH OF THE DRIVE-IN

F or weeks the utmost secrecy enshrouded the undertaking," read the newspaper reports. They were describing the last-minute preparations for a new enterprise about to be attempted near Camden in South Jersey in 1933. The clandestine approach was out of fear that someone might steal the idea before the patents had been secured. The inventor and his lawyer had filed back on August 6, 1932, and when approval for Patent No. 1,909,537 arrived on May 16, 1933, Richard M. Hollingshead Jr. of Riverton, New Jersey, was ready to introduce the motoring public to the latest exciting development in America's growing love affair with the automobile.

While the first automobiles worthy of the term came out of Europe, America seized on the technology with true gusto. The mass-production methods introduced by Ransom Olds in 1902 and expanded on by Henry Ford in 1914 brought the contraptions within reach of more than just the wealthy in search of a toy. This profitable egalitarianism propelled the United States into the emerging auto industry, and few technologies would so dramatically reshape the American landscape and culture—whether this was for the better or worse has been subject to debate ever since.

Between 1920 and 1930, the number of cars on the roads per one thousand Americans jumped from 87 to 217. (In 2009, it was just over 808.) This nearly two-and-a-half-fold spike in new motorists came with a demand for new auto-friendly services of both the practical and novelty varieties. Among the former, of course, would be establishing better-marked and paved roads. Colored bands painted on telephone poles identified early "auto trails" set

La Vérité

En lisant une annonce, bien entendu toujours louangeuse, on a tendance à l'accuser d'exagération et à prévoir une déception possible.

Ayez confiance dans la publicité Ford. Lorsque vous y lisez que la Ford est une voiture élégante, pratique, sans pareille sur le marché mondial vu son prix, quant à sa qualité, sa facilité de conduite, sa souplesse et la modicité de son entretien, ce sont là faits patents, prouvés par plus de 13 millions de véhicules sortis des usines Ford.

Allez voir la dernière création Ford, essayez-la; ce que nous en disons n'est que l'expression de la vérité.

Ford

Automobiles Ford, S. A., 225, Quai Aulagnier
Asnières (Seine)
AGENTS DANS TOUTE LA FRANCE
Pour tous achats, traitez toujours directement avec l'un de nos 2000 Agents ou Garagistes Officiels.

Ford's mass-production techniques brought the automobile to the average person all over the world. This 1926 ad appeared in a French magazine.

up by private—and not always reputable—business concerns. Maintenance wasn't always a priority, and the job was adopted on the state or local level. By 1925, the federal government recognized the advantages of a national roadway system, and its American Association of State Highway Officials (AASHO) began establishing the protocol for numbered highways, to be maintained by the states. This would continue to 1956, when the Interstate Highway System was formed.

Traditionalists lamented how this newfound mechanical freedom to up and venture great distances would erode our sense of "community." But it also presented folks with the opportunity to travel and see parts of the nation they might otherwise never get to visit. Aside from roads, the ability to refuel and find overnight lodgings extended the automobile's reach globally. The very first "filling station" was set up at a pharmacy in Wiesloch, Germany, in 1888. In America, motorists could stop at general stores, hardware stores and, ironically, even blacksmith shops to top off their tanks. The first purpose-built gas station was constructed in St. Louis, Missouri, in 1905.

At first, long-distance drivers who couldn't afford fancy hotels just pulled off onto the side of a road and slept in their vehicles. Others brought tents and camped by their cars. They made makeshift kitchens and beds or bought one of the new towable campers that began appearing on the market. Campsite businesses that could offer amenities on the cheap, such as running water, restrooms and picnic grounds, started welcoming weary motorists to their "auto camps." These evolved into "tourist courts," consisting of stand-alone cabins with overhangs to protect the car. Linking these cabins together and sharing utility infrastructures made sense, and soon was born the motel—hotels oriented for the motoring tourist, offering hotel-like services. There is a simple way to tell if it's a motel or a hotel—look where the room doors communicate into. If they open into an interior hallway, it's a hotel. If they open to the outside—for easy access to your car—it's a motel.

By the 1930s, the automobile wasn't merely a mode of transportation—it was a lifestyle. The car was a centerpiece of a modern, cosmopolitan existence, where the driver dashed from here to there in style. Catering to this busy life was the concept of the "drive-in" or "drive-through," where one didn't even have to get out of his car while running errands. In contrast to the then seemingly passé idea of a sit-down meal, the on-the-go motorist could pull into a drive-in restaurant, where the waiters and waitresses came to you—sometimes even on roller skates—and you ate right there in your car. Kirby's Pig Stand, in Dallas, Texas, was the first in 1921, but drive-ins became iconic of American youth culture through the 1950s all over the nation.

Periodically, truly strange drive-in or through-businesses have popped up over the years—from drive-through funeral parlors to Pennsylvania legislator Kevin P. Murphy's drive-through consultation window at his office. So-called safari parks opened, where visitors drove their cars through fenced parks containing wild animals in a variation on the traditional zoo. Many were novelties or fads that never quite caught on, but we still appreciate the convenience offered by drive-through windows at fast-food restaurants and do our banking at drive-up windows or ATMs. Some, such as drive-in restaurants, are even making a nostalgic comeback.

But Mr. Hollingshead's 1933 patent was about to marry two emerging pop-culture technologies.

Outdoor Movies

Even in hard times, there are certain vices Americans are loathe to give up. Richard Milton Hollingshead Jr. was careful to take that into account when he was seeking to make his own career path in his early thirties. Born on February 25, 1900, he had been working with his father's company, where he probably learned to pay attention to such things. Richard Hollingshead Sr. started making soap in his kitchen sink in Millville, New Jersey, used for cleaning horse harnesses. He was successful enough to move operations to Camden, but he understood what the rise of the horseless carriage meant for his business. Fortunately, it was the kind of product that could be easily transitioned, and he was soon selling cleaners for cars under the name of the Whiz Auto Products Company.

Also a student of trends, Richard Jr. understood that whatever business he went into, it had to be cash-in-hand—the nation was starting to slide into the Great Depression (the stock market had just crashed on October 29, 1929), and he knew credit would be too much of a risk in such times. He also understood that the collective belt-tightening would lead to the public skimping on certain spending. So he sat down and tried to work out where people would be the least likely to cut their budgets. In an interesting statement on human nature, he found many were more apt to trim their food and clothing expenditures than their cars or going to the movies.

His first thoughts were a bit grandiose. He envisioned a Hawaiian-themed gas station, complete with a faux-thatched roof and pumps disguised as palm trees, while patrons having their cars serviced could wait at a restaurant or outdoor movie theater. But he soon pared that down to the combination of automobiles and movies. True to form, he did more market research, asking for all the things about the existing indoor movie houses that turned off the potential moviegoer. It was a time when going to the movies was just beginning to turn from being a special event into a commonplace experience. It was also an era where people were expected to get dressed up when they went out to the picture shows, adding more time and bother. Then there was what to do about the kids—arranging for a babysitter was expensive, and misbehavior made them an embarrassing nuisance to fellow moviegoers. Cramped seats were uncomfortable and the bane of the portly. Indeed, there is a story of suspicious credibility that Hollingshead's mother was a large lady, and it was her irritation with the small seats that inspired her son.

Ah, Hollingshead realized, but what if the patron *never had to even get out of his or her car?* What if he added the movie experience to the growing list of "drive-in" entertainments? You could wear what you wanted, closed windows would contain the kids' noise and seating would be comparatively plush and roomy regardless of one's body type. Heck, you could even smoke (there were bans on smoking in indoor theaters). You could munch on snacks and slurp your drinks to your heart's content.

Thinking things through, however, he understood it was more than just a projector in a parking lot; there were technical considerations to work out. So, Hollingshead began conducting his secretive experiments at his home at 212 Thomas Avenue in Riverton, New Jersey. The neighborhood is still thick with trees, which no doubt helped, but one has to wonder what a nosey neighbor might have thought had they seen the strange experiments. He began by placing his Kodak projector on the hood of his car, projecting onto a sheet nailed across some trees. A radio speaker was put behind the sheet to see how the sound might work. But where it would have really appeared odd to that theoretical nosey neighbor was when he turned on the lawn-sprinkler to mimic rain conditions. Then he hoisted the front end of the car up on blocks—he was trying to get the angles right for a terrace of inclined stalls, so the cars wouldn't obstruct the view of the row behind them. His attention to detail even envisioned inclined entrance and exit ramps that would permit a latecomer or early leaver to coast in or out without the distraction to others of running their engines.

Such an enterprise was only ever going to be as profitable as how many carloads of paying customers could fit for a given show. He settled on a ratio of a five-hundred-foot-long lot and a fifty-foot-wide screen—a screen far bigger than was typical for indoor theaters. And that meant the need for a projector that could project an image bright enough to cover the distance—what's called a projector's "throw." A screen-maker, however, was secured that could supply both. He even thought of how insects would naturally be attracted by the brilliant projection light, casting shadows onto the screen. Fans would play a constant stream of air before the lens to shoo them away. Everything seemed to have been falling into place, but one key element would prove a little tougher.

Ever since the 1920s, movie patrons had come to expect recorded sound with their films. But indoor theaters had walls and ceilings—and longstanding acoustic science experience on how to use them to bounce sound to the back rows even in the days before electronic amplification. Translating that to the great outdoors was a challenge. The space was larger, and there was more ambient noise with which to compete. Volume alone wasn't the answer—the rows nearest the speakers would be blasted, and that certainly wouldn't win the theater any friends in the neighborhood. Fortunately for Hollingshead, however, the answer was next door to his father's business in Camden.

Since 1901, the Victor Talking Machine Company had grown into the world's first recording industry giant. Becoming RCA Victor in 1929, it grew into the largest manufacturer of both phonographs and phonograph recordings in the world. Among the voices preserved by the Camden studios was Enrico Caruso. RCA was the leader at the time in the cutting-edge audio technology, and it accepted the challenge of creating the sound system for this new outdoor theater.

What it came up with was called "controlled directional sound." Three speakers would focus the sound waves, confining them to the theater's environs. An early version of surround sound, they could spread an even soundscape across the lot. The system was considered enough of an innovation to be highlighted in the subsequent press.

A former architectural draftsman with the Victor Talking Machine Company was hired to design and draw up the plans. Howard E. Hall had worked for Victor between 1920 and 1926 and was an established architect in the Camden area.

After all that work to come up with an optimal plan, Hollingshead understood he had to protect his idea with a patent. So he hired a lawyer, Leonard Kalish, to handle the paperwork and applications. In the meantime, he pitched the idea to his cousin, Willie Warren Smith, who owned parking lots in Camden, New York and Philadelphia. Smith bought in, and together they formed Park-In Theatres, Inc. They traded stock in the new company for the services of Edward Ellis, a contractor who did the road-grading work. Stock was also bought by Oliver Willets, the vice-president of Camden's other industrial powerhouse, Campbell Soup.

When the patent was approved on May 16, 1933, Hollingshead and his team were ready to hit the ground running. Finding the manpower to construct a theater was easy enough, but the hard times brought an added complication. Men were eager for the relief of even a temporary construction job and, at first, accepted the twenty cents an hour for unskilled labor and forty cents for skilled. It still had more dignity than being on the Pennsauken Township relief rolls. Labor unions were watching, however, trying to get the best deals possible for such desperate men and their families. They showed up to demand forty cents for unskilled and $1.40 for skilled. There is an inherent tension between unions looking out for the interests of their members and managements looking to maximize profits by cutting costs. But with the Great Depression looming, the pressures were all the more acute. In his 1993 history of drive-ins, cultural historian Kerry Segrave describes how it got bad enough to cause fistfights on the site, sending two men to the hospital. "In some fashion, the deadlock was broken," he writes, "and even with the labor problems, construction was completed in less than three weeks."

Wife Beware

Hollingshead and his partners likely eyed the weather reports with concern leading up to opening night. They weren't necessarily worrying about rain—his lawn sprinkler experiments had proven the show could go on, though it is questionable how many people would come out in bad weather. Snow might shut them down, of course, but cold weather was becoming less of an issue; heaters of various degrees of efficiency were common enough in cars since the 1920s, and in 1933 Ford unveiled the first in-dash heater. But what they were dealing with during that early June was near-hundred-degree temperatures and high humidity. Factory-installed air conditioners wouldn't appear in cars until the 1940 Packard. AC was a marketing advantage for the indoor theaters, which could offer patrons relief when most homes relied on fans at best.

It was a muggy eighty-seven degrees on June 6, 1933, as the first drive-in theater in history flickered to life for paying patrons. This entertainment first is most often described as being a bragging right for Camden. But as Segrave pointed out, that technically isn't correct. The exact site lay just across the border in Pennsauken Township, where Admiral Wilson Boulevard becomes Crescent Boulevard. Given the proximity to the better-known city, it probably just made sense to tell everyone it was in Camden rather than explain where Pennsauken was.

The evening's entertainment was *Wife Beware*, a 1932 British comedy. Adolphe Menjou starred as an unhappily married philandering rogue who fakes amnesia to establish a new life as a car salesman before being discovered by a friend of his (unknown to him) pregnant wife. Dismissed by one critic as "an unpleasant little comedy, despite a strong cast," it was not really Hollingshead's fault that they got a second-run mediocre movie. Distributors were leery of helping undercut their traditional indoor theaters in favor of this experiment in novelty. This would continue to be an issue for drive-in theaters for years to come, as if the industry had a hard time taking them completely seriously.

Patrons were charged a quarter for the car and a quarter per person. Vehicles with four people or more were admitted for a flat dollar. While the

Adolphe Menjou (shown here in 1956 with Myrna Loy) was the star of the first movie shown at a drive-in theater, 1932's *Wife Beware.*

theater was nearly sold out, some stalls were filled by the media from nearby Philadelphia and Camden that received free passes. There were spots for four hundred cars—an average of four people per car could yield audiences as large as 1,600—on a 250,000-square-foot lot that the ushers used bicycles to cover. Trees and a wall helped both contain the sound and prevent someone from just standing outside and watching for free. Estimates of how much it all cost range from a likely exaggerated $60,000 to a more typical $25,000 to $30,000. A week after opening, a concessions stand was added. Where indoor moviegoers got popcorn and candy, the drive-in offered beer and more complete meals, trying to gain an advantage.

Attendance dropped the rest of the week, likely because of the heat and humidity. The response of the news media to the event is hard to gauge. Segrave characterizes reports as more "matter-of-fact" than enthusiastic. Some did appear to damn the idea with faint praise, printing only short filler pieces perfunctorily stating it had opened. Others went into more detail, citing statistics and a list of advantages likely taken directly from Hollingshead's own promotions. A Baton Rouge, Louisiana newspaper, the *Advocate,* for example, declared the new drive-ins "will be hailed by the motoring public and the people who don't care to dress for their evening's entertainment." What seemed so obvious to its creator wasn't as intuitive for others. The *Motion Picture Herald* openly asked the natural question, "Why is it desirable to remain in your automobile when you go to the movies?" The *Literary Digest* questioned if people would really want to trade the intimacy of an indoor theater for the convenience of a drive-in and pondered the effects of weather. C.E. Butterfield, writing for the Associated Press, however, described how "on one occasion during an electrical and rain storm, the show went right on, losing only three cars—of the open type."

Some reports were less skeptical, if not enthused. California's *Riverside Daily Press* put it on the front page of its September 14, 1933 edition, complete with an illustration and diagram of how the inclined parking worked. *Popular Mechanics* magazine included it along with illustrations as well. But the consensus was that it was an interesting enough novelty—worth reporting, certainly—but not exactly the wave of the future of cinema. Indeed, on the outskirts of the industry was where they would remain.

That wasn't without some reason. For all of Hollingshead's careful planning, there were still technical problems that hurt the idea's allure as a long-term enterprise. Fitting enough cars per row to make it pay meant those on the ends had an oblique, distorted view of the screen. As much as the sound system was innovative, the time it took the sound waves to reach some distances caused it to be out of sync with the movie for some patrons. The latter would, of course, be solved with the individual speaker systems that came later. But the technology wasn't yet quite up to the scale needed.

Beyond that, however, was the annoying resistance from mainstream Hollywood to provide first-run products from the major studios. True, there were independents that were only too happy to find any outlet, but most people weren't willing to spend that kind of money on obscure or second-rate entertainment—especially when indoor theaters offered double-bills of first-run movies from major studios at an average of twenty-three cents a ticket. Not having to dress up just wasn't enough of an incentive.

The first drive-in movie theater lasted just two or three years, until Hollingshead sold it to a man from Union Township who ran several indoor theaters. When describing the end, Kerry Segrave intentionally placed the word "moved" in quotes—it isn't clear if the sale was just for the concept or if any of the physical equipment went to Union. In any case, the Union Drive-In opened on Route 22 East, billing itself as "America's most modern drive-in theater." It expanded to a 1,400-car capacity and included a playground for the kids, as well as the traditional concessions stand. Even though it survived to 1983, its novelty just couldn't overcome the limitations of summer-only hours and the lure of multiplex theaters.

Richard Hollingshead maintained that the Camden Theater wasn't a failure, blaming its demise on the high cost of even the second-run films. *Wives Beware*, he later claimed, had cost them $400 for four days, where a South Camden indoor theater rented it for just $20 a day.

He held on to a 30 percent interest in his Park-In Theatres Company, hoping to make a living off licensing fees from his patent. By 1953, it was reportedly doing business in 193 countries, but the profits were never enough. It wasn't that there were not people interested in the concept, but rather that they wanted to make changes that sometimes led to questions of patent infringements. The industry became mired in litigations. Hollingshead might not have been able to sit back and rake in the profits from licensing fees, but he wasn't left destitute either. As early as 1934, he had gone back to working for his father, inheriting the company and becoming its chairman of the board in 1950. He retired to Villanova, Pennsylvania, in 1964 and passed away from cancer on May 13, 1975.

If Richard Hollingshead wasn't bitter about how things worked out, Laura Ottinger was. She had hired on as his secretary in 1953 and felt it had been keenly unfair that he never received credit from Hollywood for his contribution to the industry. She even regularly nagged the Academy of Motion Picture Arts and Sciences during the 1970s in an unsuccessful bid to get her old boss a posthumous Academy Award. She argued that he had kept the industry going during the dark days of the Great Depression, but as Kerry Segrave points out, that was something of an overstatement. Drive-ins were still too few and far between, and Americans—true to the pattern Hollingshead had noticed—were happy to spend their meager money on the chance to slip into a darkened movie house and escape their woes for a little while. But she was correct in a sense. When smaller theaters were shuttering up in droves in the 1950s as televisions began flickering in an increasing number of living rooms, drive-ins proved rather resilient to the onslaught. It could be argued that they helped keep cinema relevant.

Segrave related a funny story from an interview with Hollingshead shortly before his death. He and his wife occasionally still went to the Main Line Drive-in not far from where they lived. When asked what kinds of movies he liked to see there, he said with a chuckle, "I like the dirty movies best."

Chapter 3

TRENTON MAKES—THE WORLD TAKES... ELECTRIC CHAIRS!

If you have ever driven up New Jersey's Route 29 along the Delaware River into Trenton, you've probably seen the huge neon letters attached to the Warren Street Bridge as its trusses arch over into Pennsylvania. Installed in 1935, they make the declaration: "Trenton Makes—The World Takes."

These days, after years of decline in American manufacturing, such oversized boasting seems a tad ironic. Yet much of the city's history is indeed deeply rooted in industrial prowess. It was, for example, Trenton's furnaces that kept American troops supplied with critical iron during the Revolution. Most people will at least be vaguely aware of the Roebling name—think Brooklyn Bridge—whose factories were in Trenton. At the height of its industrial might, the city's factories churned out everything from rubber and wire rope to ceramics and cigars.

But what might come as a surprise—a jolt, one might say—is that amongst the products Trenton made for the world to take was electric chairs.

The Death Penalty

The idea of putting a criminal to death has been part of communal systems of justice for as long as there have been records of crimes and punishments. As might be expected, such an extreme response was intuitively reserved for that most egregious of antisocial behaviors: murder. But over the centuries,

The crucifixion of Jesus Christ has become central to the iconography of Christianity but was a common form of execution of the time. Sainte Bible, *1866, drawn by Gustave Doré, engraved by J. Gauchard Brunier.*

various societies have expanded the list of eligible offences in accordance with respective perceptions of societal norms and taboos. Sexual transgressions such as rape and incest have been included, for example, but also adultery and homosexuality. Governments soon learned to protect themselves against dissent by including treason as a capital offence. Militaries have long used pain of death as a means to deter desertion or insubordination.

The means invented for dispatching the condemned make up an unsettling if creative list: burning at the stake, the breaking wheel, stoning, crushing, drawing and quartering, slow slicing, disemboweling, impalement, dismemberment, et cetera. But perhaps the most obvious example of early capital punishment has become so ubiquitous in Western culture that we often don't see it for what it actually depicts. The central emblem in Christian iconography is the crucifix. Whether it's a literal depiction of Christ suffering on a wooden cross or the abstract cross shape alone, it was symbolic of a form of capital punishment common in the Roman Empire. While not exclusively Roman—or even always involving the cross shape—the basic idea of affixing someone to a structure and leaving him to slowly die brings up an important aspect to our story. Capital and corporal punishment were one and the same. The point was to make the condemned *suffer* first. There is a fine line between a sense of revenge and a sense of justice, and a quick death didn't seem as great a punishment as dragging out the agony.

But there was more to it than that. Public executions put the suffering on display, perhaps acting as a deterrent to anyone in the crowd contemplating the same behaviors that brought such horrors on the condemned. There is some question, of course, about just how much of a deterrent any such punishments really are—after all, people still commit crimes regardless. And public executions often became more macabre entertainment than moral lesson.

Certainly, though, in the face of some horrific crime, there is something collectively cathartic in the grim satisfaction that comes from seeing the guilty suffer—again, that fine line between revenge and justice. Nevertheless, social critics have long suggested that by indulging such base desires for vengeance, we dilute our claim to being "civilized." On the other hand, execution can be argued as a legitimate defense of civilization against degradation from the most egregiously uncivilized acts. A sort of middle ground has been established that divorces corporal punishment from capital. In this view, execution becomes an acceptable penalty for specific crimes, but making the condemned suffer first through torture is not.

This idea is embodied in the concept of "cruel and unusual punishment." The phrase dates back at least as far as 1689, when it was worked into the English Bill of Rights and was later adopted in the United States Constitution's Eighth Amendment: "Excessive bail shall not be required, nor excessive fines imposed, nor cruel and unusual punishments inflicted."

But exactly what constitutes "cruel and unusual" has been subject to debate and left to be hashed out in courts. The basic definition is any punishment that causes undue suffering or humiliation or does not fit the degree of the crime. Still, "undue suffering" is somewhat subjective. Anti-capital punishment advocates assert that execution is, in and of itself, cruel and unusual. Nevertheless, if one were to accept that a death penalty is an acceptable punishment, the issue then becomes how to carry that out in a manner that isn't unduly cruel. The emotional distress between hearing the sentence and it being carried out notwithstanding, the final act of death should happen as quickly and painlessly as possible—in other words, as "humanely" as possible.

Cultures have experimented with a range of execution methods, each thought to reasonably meet the criteria of being humane. Decapitation was long used as a seemingly quick and painless means. A good sharp blade and an accurate swing can get the job done quickly and, presumably, with little suffering. The problem in practice, however, has been human error—a poorly aimed swing. There are historic examples of multiple swings being required—to the presumed extreme distress of the condemned. When the guillotine was introduced in France, it sought to mechanize the process, better-removing the human factor. But even when it was swift and accurate, there were still accounts—albeit anecdotal—of severed heads exhibiting movements that hinted that death was perhaps not quite as immediate as believed. Nevertheless, France used the guillotine right up to 1981, when it abolished the death penalty.

A firing squad might seem a reasonable alternative. Paintings of Saint Sebastian usually depict him being executed by Roman archers in 228, so the idea is not a new one. But here again, it is subject to the accuracy of the shooters. Still, a firing squad was employed as late as 2010 in Utah, where the condemned had specifically requested it. Given the ubiquity of weapons on the battlefield, firing squads have always been an expedient for military executions.

But perhaps the most iconic emblem of execution has been the hangman's noose and gallows. Done properly, the condemned drops quickly and the noose snaps the neck, bringing death before the person is aware it's happening—"done properly" being the operative phrase. Too short of a drop and the person chokes, flailing about in clear distress. Too long and an unintended beheading can occur.

Despite the potential for such grisly outcomes, hanging had become the preferred method of "humane" state executions in the United States until the start of the twentieth century, when a new means seemed to hold more promise.

The Electric Chair

The nineteenth-century industrial revolution had been the domain of King Coal and his Age of Steam. But as the twentieth century dawned, the king faced dethroning by the emergence of practical electricity. Ever since the first hominid stared up in awe at a lightning storm, the idea of tapping into that raw energy had enthralled and taunted humanity. It even featured in the American creation myth—Benjamin Franklin and his kite remain part of our national iconography, though it is doubtful he ever really carried out

Benjamin Franklin's alleged "kite experiment" is questioned by historians but has remained part of American folklore.

that specific experiment. When Mary Shelly needed a force by which her Dr. Frankenstein could animate the dead corps, she had him pulling lightning from the skies—a compelling enough image that it has become a classic staple of the mad scientist in horror movies.

The end of the nineteenth century saw, at last, an understanding of the physics of electricity that had matured enough to enable generating it on the grand scale. Industrialists like Edison and Westinghouse saw the economic potential of electricity and began wrapping the republic in an ever-expanding web of wires. The 1893 World's Columbian Exhibition, held in Chicago, dazzled visitors with displays of the then still-novel electric light.

This was the future. New appliances came on the market, and even old ones were improved, promising to remove the drudgery from everyday life. In the early twentieth century, if it was modern, progressive and hip, it was electric.

That electricity could also be dangerous, however, certainly wasn't unknown. Remember Ben Franklin and his kite? While he did dabble in experiments with electric current, historians debate if the kite in a lightning storm wasn't just one of the literary pranks he was known for indulging in. One man, however, certainly took it seriously—to his ultimate peril. Georg Richmann, a Swedish physicist at the Imperial Court of St. Petersburg in Russia, attempted to replicate Franklin's alleged lightning rod experiments in 1753. Unfortunately, he was killed when he failed to properly insulate

Georg Richmann, a Swedish physicist at the Imperial Court of St. Petersburg in Russia, attempted to replicate Franklin's alleged lightning rod experiments in 1753 but was killed when he failed to properly insulate himself.

himself. By the turn of the last century, however, the evolution of the electrician had evolved from amateur experimenter to professional trade, bringing with it safe standard practices passed along through apprenticeship systems and labor unions and enforced with licensing.

Nevertheless, of course, accidents did happen, often with tragic results. In 1881, so the story goes, a dentist from Buffalo, New York, Dr. Alfred Southwick, happened to witness just such an accident. An inebriated man touched a live electric generator, killing himself—quickly and painlessly, it seemed. This set the good doctor thinking. Maybe this brave new electrified world could also lead to civilization being able to apply its most severe perception of justice in a more humane and urbane manner.

Southwick was among those enamored with all things electric and had followed developments in the field, believing they would have application in dentistry. He noted, for example, the numbing effect of low voltage current and pondered its value as an anesthetic. Also excited about electricity was a fellow Buffalo doctor, George Fell, with whom Southwick shared his ideas at a local scientific society conference. Both being on the same page, they went to the head of the Buffalo Society for the Prevention of Cruelty to Animals. Up to then, there had been a certain irony in the name: unwanted animals were drowned in a bucket. That the society was killing animals whose only crime was homelessness wasn't in question. As with condemned humans, the issue was how it was carried out. Electrocution, the doctors convinced the society, was more efficient and humane. It also gave them a supply of unfortunate creatures on which to experiment. The goal was to create an apparatus that would work on humans.

Being a dentist, it is assumed Southwick designed a *chair* for the condemned rather than a table or other form. When it came time to build the final design, the choice was perhaps as obvious as it was limited. Thomas Edison had become world famous for his development of a practical electric light bulb (he did not invent the light bulb). Around the time Southwick and Fell were conducting their grim experiments, Edison was engaged in a spirited war with George Westinghouse over whether the nation would be run on AC or DC current. While Edison and his DC current would ultimately lose that battle, it would be to Edison's New Jersey factory that Southwick would turn. Edison himself is sometimes credited with building the first electric chair. While work was done with his blessing and promotional skills, it was in fact two of his employees, Harold P. Brown and Arthur Kennelly, who did the hands-on labor. Kennelly was chief engineer at Edison's West Orange, New Jersey facility.

Building an electrocution apparatus was one thing. Getting a state to adopt it as its means of execution was another. Fortunately for Southwick, he counted among his powerful friends a strong defender of the death penalty against those who sought its abolishment. New York State senator Daniel H. McMillan saw in Southwick's plan a way of dealing a blow to the logic of the anti–capital punishment argument. If electrocution was indeed quick and painless, it could no longer be claimed that it inflicted undue suffering— or that it met the legal definitions for "cruel and unusual." McMillan made sure that Southwick's proposal was placed on the desk of New York's then governor, David Bennett Hill, with his support. The timing was fortuitous for Hill. In his 1885 State of the State address, he had charged the legislature with the task of finding a way to take the life of the condemned in a less barbarous manner. And here was the very means to do it.

In 1886, Hill appointed a three-man Commission to Investigate and Report the Most Humane and Practical Method of Carrying into Effect the Sentence of Death in Capital Cases. Dr. Southwick was on the panel, along with Matthew Hale and Elbridge Gerry, and not surprisingly, they recommended in their 1888 report that the state adopt electrocution to replace hanging in New York State. A bill was introduced to amend the Criminal Procedure Code accordingly but met mixed reactions from both politicians and the public. It lingered and limped through several eviscerating amendments until it seemed as doomed as the convicts it would impact. Then, on May 8, 1888, during the last day of the legislative session, Senator Henry Coggleshell used what has been described as political gymnastics to restore the language to its original form and get passage by a voice vote. Signed into law by Governor Hill on June 5, it established that on January 1, 1889, New York would become the first state to adopt electrocution as the means to carry out capital punishment.

They didn't have to wait very long for their first opportunity to try it out on a human being. On March 29, 1889, William Kemmler murdered

A contemporary newspaper illustration of William Kemmler, the first man to be executed in an electric chair in 1889.

his common-law wife, Tillie Ziegler, with a hatchet. Found guilty, he was sentenced to the dubious honor of being the first man to die in the electric chair on August 6, 1889, at New York's Auburn Prison. At first, it all seemed to go as planned. Kemmler was calm as he took the seat and received one thousand volts. The attending doctor pronounced him dead.

And then someone noticed that the man was still breathing.

Confirming this, the doctor was said to have called out, "Have the current turned on again, quick—no delay!" The problem was, however, there would indeed be a delay. If he was at all conscious, Kemmler would have endured some eight minutes waiting for the generator to charge back up sufficiently. The second jolt did the job but caused blood vessels to burst and bleed. The flesh around the electrodes singed, producing a smell that led some witnesses to wonder if he had actually caught fire. The next day's headlines screamed the sensational story of what amounted to a botched execution. George Westinghouse later quipped, "They would have done better using an axe." While he perhaps had a point, he was also miffed that the state used the direct current (DC) championed by his rival, Edison.

Dr. Southwick, who was present, had a very different reaction, despite the obvious glitches. He was reported as having proclaimed, "There is the culmination of ten years work and study! We live in a higher civilization from this day."

Adams Electrical Company

It is, of course, subject to debate whether Kemmler was indeed some sort of sacrifice to the dawn of a "higher civilization." But what it did mark was how states with death penalties would begin the shift from the noose to the electron—and the emergence of a new industry to provide the machinery that facilitated it.

Capital punishment had been part of New Jersey's penal system since the early colonial period. The earliest extant record of someone being sentenced to death is for a Negro slave named Tom, who was hanged in Monmouth County for rape in 1690. Indeed, of the thirty-four people executed between 1690 and 1749 in New Jersey, twenty-four were black, six white, three unknown (not recorded) and one Native American. All were male, except for one woman and one unrecorded. The majority were convicted of murder, with some robbery, horse stealing, counterfeiting and at least one "slave revolt." The hangman claimed all but six, who were burned at the stake (including the one woman, a slave named Sherron Hager, for murder in 1717 in Salem County). The last to be condemned to burning was a male slave in 1752 for a murder in Somerset County. After that, all were hanged until the start of the twentieth century.

In 1907, the state legislature passed the bills necessary to make electrocution the preferred means, and it fell to the head of the state prison in Trenton to arrange for the necessary apparatus to be installed. The Keeper, as he was known, at the time was George O. Osborne. Born in 1845 in Elmira, New York, he came to the attention of the governor for his work as warden of a hospital in Jersey City. On March 5, 1902, Governor Franklin Murphy appointed him Keeper. Later newspaper photographs show a man with heavy eyes and fluffy whiskers. Within a month of taking the post, Osborne had his first execution of murderer George Hettrick on April 4, by hanging.

Osborne probably took to the idea of electrocution as a more humane method since he would become known for being reform minded, trying to modernize New Jersey's prison system. But while electrocution was becoming the standard, an electric chair wasn't exactly an off-the-shelf kind of purchase. He needed someone who could make him one from scratch. The most

obvious place to begin was calling in an expert: an electrician. Carl F. Adams, who would later be described as a man of ponderous reserve, good nerves and calm temper of mind, seemed a logical enough choice. Born in 1868, he was the founder of Adams Electrical Company and had already earned a good reputation around Trenton.

The increasingly widespread availability of electric power meant there was a reasonable trade to be found in installing

This photo of Carl F. Adams appeared with his obituary in several newspapers. The glasses and receding hairline seem to belie the fact that his products were designed to kill condemned prisoners.

electric lighting, particularly on commercial properties. In 1897, Carl F. Adams, identified as an electrical engineer and contractor, had been awarded the contract to light the new addition to the Trenton Fire Clay and Porcelain Company. The *Trenton Evening Times* reported that "[w]hen completed there will be about 750 lights of 16-candle power." He had already installed the lighting on the existing older building the previous winter.

The next year, he published notice that he moved from 103 East State Street to 16 East State Street, including an office, supply department and "first-class repair shop." By 1901, he also had a factory on Hamilton Street, manufacturing "the Backus motor fans...This is the only plant of its kind in the city," according to the *Trenton Evening Times*. By 1903, he had begun getting jobs for the City of Trenton itself, including wiring a new firehouse on Broad Street.

But the road to that meeting with the warden was paved by higher-profile jobs. In 1903, his company was hired to install the electric lighting at the Trent Theatre. But it was probably a job at the statehouse the following year that got him the most attention. It had been noticed that the chandelier hanging in the rotunda always swung, even when it wasn't windy. That in and of itself wasn't an issue. But when the maintenance people took a closer look, they realized that there was nothing in how it was constructed to permit the flexibility demanded by that natural swinging, causing dangerous wear. In other words, it might come crashing down at any moment, and people who worked in the building after a while learned to walk quickly when they had to cross the rotunda space. Adams was hired in October 1904 to take it down and replace it with a modern electric light chandelier.

As an aside, local theater owner I.C. Mishler, who owned the State Theatre in Trenton, bought the old chandelier and had it installed—with safety improvements—at another theater he had opened in Altoona, Pennsylvania. Sadly, it was destroyed as part of a huge fire that consumed not only the theater but also an Elks Home and the Oliver Robert furniture store, with an estimated $500,000 in damages.

Not that it was all smooth sailing for the Adams Electrical Company. Adams was frequently at odds with the labor unions involved with the electrical trade. Indeed, the statehouse job was delayed by a dispute with the Building Trades Council. Adams had an eye toward an "open shop"—non-union. Ten union workers walked off the job as a protest against the use of non-union labor. This would pit Adams against the council well into February 1905.

One of the striking electricians, Albert Hutloff, was short on cash to support his family. So he picked up a small job at a house on the west side of town for E.M. Fleron, a competitor of Adams. This irked Adams, as there was supposed to be a gentleman's agreement that no contractor would hire the strikers. Fleron, in turn, wasn't very happy with Adams and accused him of trying to intimidate Hutloff into quitting the extra job.

The Building Trades Council was playing for keeps as well. It called a strike for six of its members who had been working for Adams. Five walked off the job, but one stayed. He was immediately kicked out of the organization, and it vowed to boycott Adams entirely, throwing its full support behind the other men who were on strike. Adams had intended to become an open shop by April 1 but retaliated by locking out the union workers in January 1905. Three construction jobs ground to a halt around Trenton—at the Second Regiment Armory, the home of C.C. Haven and the Second Presbyterian Church—because of labor unrest with the Building Trades Council. In the case of the armory, the problem was the presence of a worker who belonged to the National Association of Steamfitters, which the American Federation of Labor did not recognize as being legitimate. "All of the large jobs now in course of construction are shunned by labor union men because of the Adams matter or the lockout of plumbers by the Master Plumbers Union," reported the *Trenton Evening Times*.

This time, however, management stuck together and responded in kind. Six electrical contractors locked out between twelve and fifteen union electricians as a result of an agreement they had all signed with the Electrical Contractors Association to have open shops. This was part of a larger protest by the Manufacturers and Employers Association against what they saw as the sympathetic strike policy of the Mercer County Building Trades Association. The irony, of course, was that the employers were organizing together for their common interests in order to protect their workers from doing the exact same thing. In any event, this time Adams wasn't directly involved since he had locked out union workers the previous month, but the newspaper reports traced the entire mess back to his initial fight.

Not that any of this seems to have hurt him. Later in 1905, he received a $262 contract to install lights for the New Jersey Supreme Court, and the following year, he created an "elaborate electrical display" at the State Street Theatre and St. Mary's Cathedral as part of the celebrations surrounding the silver jubilee of the ordination of the Reverend Monsignor John H. Fox. This was a big deal to the community, and Adams's participation was duly noted in the papers, providing free and positive publicity.

By the time New Jersey needed an electric chair, Carl F. Adams was an established businessman who had done other minor electrical work for the State Penitentiary before, making him a logical choice.

The only problem was that he had no experience whatever with such a contraption as he was now being asked to build. But he wasn't about to let that stop him.

New Jersey's Electric Chair

The obvious place to start for Adams was right in his own New Jersey backyard—with the Wizard of Menlo Park himself. Edison has gone down in pop history as something of a father to all things electrical, up there with Franklin and his kite. In reality, for example, Edison did not invent the electric light bulb—historians identify some twenty-three inventors of the incandescent light bulb going back to 1802. What Edison did do, however, was to improve on the design and materials, while taking advantage of things (like better vacuum technology) that were unavailable to earlier researchers. And he was a tireless—some might say shameless—promoter who shoved his name out before the public in a way that few others had. Regardless, Edison and his employees did have a wealth of practical experience when it came to understanding the underlying principles of physics and what kinds of equipment would be needed. The "power grid" was still new, so it wasn't merely a matter of a chair that could be plugged into an existing socket. There would be a host of materials and equipment needed in support of the chair proper, plus safety considerations that would protect operators and witnesses, as well as systems that could be as failsafe as possible. A botched execution—whether from operator error or mechanical failure—wouldn't do at all.

Adams also took a trip to Sing Sing Correctional Facility in Ossining, New York, to examine its existing chair—nicknamed with macabre humor "Old Sparky." This was the same chair that had executed Martha Place, the first woman put to death by electrocution. She was born Martha Garretson in East Millstone in Somerset County, New Jersey. After a failed first marriage, she went to work as a domestic for widower William Place in Brooklyn, New York, whom she later married. Martha seems to have been jealous of her husband's affection toward his teenage daughter, Ida. Several times the police had to be summoned to diffuse altercations. On February 7, 1898, after yet another apparent argument with Ida, Martha threw acid into the seventeen-year-old girl's face, blinding her, and then suffocated her to death. When William came home that evening, Martha attacked him with an axe, severely wounding him, but he was able to crawl away and get help. Police found Martha upstairs with gas escaping from the burners in an apparent suicide attempt. She was convicted of the murder of Ida Place and the attempted murder of William and sentenced to death on March 20, 1899.

While she wasn't the first woman to receive a death sentence, she would be the first to die in the new electric chair. This novelty rekindled debates over the ethics of executing women, no matter how awful their crimes or allegedly humane the method. Additionally, this came at a time when women's rights advocates were agitating for suffrage, adding a perhaps unexpected wrinkle to the "equal rights." Some seemed to take great pleasure in pointing out that if these women wanted to be treated equally in the rest of society, so too should they be subject to the less-desirable equity of capital punishment. The papers seemed to take great pains in describing the plain-looking Martha in unflattering terms—in contrast to the sympathy they showed a more physically attractive murderess not long before who was spared a death sentence.

There is another aspect of Martha's story, however, that engages historians even today. Her brother was supposed to have said she had been struck in the head during a sledding accident when she was twenty-three and had never been quite right after that. Could her outbursts of apparent rage—including the last deadly one—have been the result of brain damage? Doctors cleared her as sane and then Governor Theodore Roosevelt declined clemency.

Carl Adams gathered his information, researched vendors for the parts and submitted a bid to the State of New Jersey to build and install its first electric chair. In June 1907, the appropriations bill was signed, allotting $10,000 for the construction of a "new death building." Adams received $1,640 that October for his part, with the promise that it would be all ready to go within six weeks—the state had an execution scheduled for December for which wanted to use his chair.

The "death building" was an annex with six cells at one end—"death row"—and the electric chair apparatus at the other. New Jerseyans in the area protested—not over moral qualms about capital punishment but with a disgust at the idea of "the scum of other counties brought here [to be] put out of existence in the state prison in old historic Trenton."

The first person to be sent to "the chair"—"getting the chair" had by this point entered the American lexicon—was Saverio DiGiovanni, a thirty-four-year-old Italian immigrant working at a wool mill in Raritan. In September 1907, he had shot and killed Joseph Sansome for motives that were never clearly established. His trial took two days, and the jury spent just fifteen minutes to return a verdict of guilty of first-degree murder. When the judge, James Bergen, sentenced him to death by electric chair, DiGiovanni, who spoke little English, didn't react. It was only when someone interpreted the sentence that he broke down. It's hard to say what brought him to that pitiful state—or if he would have been sentenced to death today. He was described as a five-foot-five bullnecked man who had the scars of many other altercations. It is said that his mood swung between boasts that no "electric chair" could kill him and weeping over a wife and baby back in Italy.

It was a sort of Catch-22—on the one hand, having a long time between sentence and execution only draws out the agony. But on the other, time needs to be permitted for possible appeals. DiGiovanni's lawyers did indeed appeal, but Governor Edward Stokes turned them down and set the execution for December 11. Hence the rush for Adams to finish the job.

The execution took place at 5:57 a.m. without a hitch. DiGiovanni wept and prayed but offered no resistance. Approximately 2,400 volts were passed through him for a full minute. A second jolt was administered as a matter of procedure, to make certain he was indeed dead, but witnesses were pretty sure he had died instantly. His body was buried in an unmarked grave at Our Lady of Lourdes Cemetery in Hamilton.

Watching it all was Carl F. Adams, proud of his handiwork. Years later, he would recall how he felt the crime was a revolting one and that he had "no feelings for a man like that."

The Adams Electrical Company Papers

If one is going to engage in the business of making electric chairs, having "no feelings for a man like that" is a prerequisite. Still, regardless of how one feels about the death penalty, there is nonetheless something a tad unsettling about viewing it through the lens of a business. There is a collection of papers from the Adams Electrical Company pertaining to electric chair orders in the Special Collections Department of Rutgers University's Alexander Library in New Brunswick. They form a strange, yet compelling narrative. Perhaps the strangest—though it is admittedly unclear how it came to be included—is a photo of the last man to be executed in the Middlesex County jail by hanging. He is identified as Fred Lang, "who shot and killed his niece [illegible] at Burnhams[?] Corner Bonhamtown, April 20th, 1906 by shooting her in the neck."

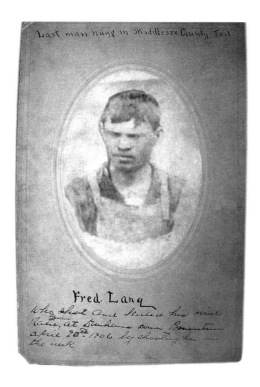

Fred Lang had the dubious distinction of having been the last condemned man to hang in Middlesex County. This picture is among the items in the collection of Adams Electric Company materials at Rutgers University's Special Collections and University Archives. *Carl F. Adams Papers, Special Collections and University Archives, Rutgers University Libraries, Ac.2399. Picture by the author.*

Fred Lang was from South Bethlehem, Pennsylvania, and he shot his niece, Ms. Gate Gordon, on April 20, 1906, at her home in Bordentown, New Jersey. She had rebuffed his proposal for marriage. It is difficult to say, but the overall-clad young man looks quite possibly to be mentally handicapped. Whatever the case, it is the remarks handwritten, albeit not completely legible, in pencil on the back that are most strange: "From M. Yuro[?] To My Dear Friend ('Pickel') 1927."

What an odd gift for someone you could call "Pickel."

Much of the rest of the collection is paperwork that would perhaps be tedious were it not for electric chairs. But it demonstrates how, following the successes at New Jersey, state after state that had death penalties began to explore passing laws abolishing hanging in favor of electrocution. The Trenton job was not to be a one-off project—electric chairs and their apparatus were going to be a new product line for the busy electrical company.

Keeper George Osborne had been pleased enough with Adams's work to recommend him. When E.F. Morgan, superintendent of the Virginia penitentiary, applied to Osborne for guidance in getting an electric chair for his state in 1908, Osborne sent him straight to Adams. Just three months after the first execution in Trenton, Adams was being asked to submit a bid in Virginia. Perhaps they would have preferred to give the contract to someone from their own state, but it was hard to argue with Adams's practical experience and rave reviews. Evidently, Morgan was invited to come and visit the Trenton facility, and Adams was shrewd enough to make certain the press knew of this unusual trip. "On my arrival at my office I find the copies of the *Daily State Gazette*," Morgan wrote back to Adams, "with a very complimentary notice of my visit to your city, for which please accept my thanks." Schmoozing aside, Adams's price evidently also impressed Virginia, as Morgan was pleased to tell him that the state board "gave you the contract, and would be glad to have you begin work at your earliest convenience."

The deal cost $3,700 with the terms of one-third cash with the order, one-third upon delivery, $500 when machine was ready for operation and the balance after the first execution. That last bit caused Adams a small grief when, by August 28, 1908, he wrote to Morgan:

> *I expected to be called to Richmond before this time by you, but apparently there are no one as yet to pay the death penalty in the Electric Chair. Kindly let me know if you can, when I may expect a check for the balance. You thought that it would not be necessary for me to wait until you had a man. I have waited for some time and as the money would be very acceptable just now, I trust that you will speak to your board about it and see if they cannot let me have the balance. I assure you, whether you pay me now or later, I will be on hand when the first man goes off.*

On September 1, 1908, Morgan replied that he had "placed your letter before my Board on yesterday for their consideration. They declined to issue check, because it is such a short time before we will have an execution." Adams would have to wait until October 13 for an execution and to be paid the balance.

Evidently, it all went off without any problems. By March 27, 1909, Morgan had reported to Adams that "[w]e have five subjects for the electric chair to be executed the same day, April 30th. Please quote me price on extra helmet and leg electrode complete, and 2 extra helmet sponges."

Morgan then makes mention of a "problem" he had:

> *It is possible that you are not familiar with all the types of negro heads and consequently it has not occurred to you that there could be such wide*

departures from the normal shape, therefore I suggest that if it can be done, that the helmets be made so as to be flexible to some extent at least. Our last experience demonstrated the necessity for such an arrangement, as the current dried out the sponge on each side of the head (which was pyramidal in shape) and showed itself in sparks.

Adams replied:

We will make an extra helmet of a design which will be more flexible in order to meet your special requirements in the execution of negro criminals... We will not make any charge to you for the reason that we want you to feel perfectly satisfied in every respect and be successful with our apparatus. We also appreciate the very kind interest that you have taken in our equipment and therefore feel that it is no more than is right that we should take care of you in every detail.

If nothing else, he took care of his customers and kept up a good reputation. The market, of course, was still rather confined, so even a single displeased client could spell ruin. Each success fed another. When, on April 13, 1910, he wrote to the state penitentiary of Frankfort, Kentucky, "From current reports we notice that you [*sic*] state has passed a law substituting electrocution for hanging as the mode of inflicting the death penalty," he could refer it to both Osborne in Trenton and Morgan in Virginia for honest testimonials of "it's successful workings." Then, when Osborne heard that Pennsylvania's House of Representatives was "contemplating installation of electrocution plants," he wrote a letter of introduction for Adams to Justice Robert A. Balfour in Philadelphia on February 3, 1911, telling how "Mr. Adams, installed the electrocution plant in this State in 1907, and we have had 17 electrocutions, all being successful in every respect. I have referred him to you, and no doubt he will be able to give you valuable suggestions."

In effect, clients themselves became his most effective salesmen—when a warden somewhere needed information on how to get an electric chair, they would, naturally enough, write to fellow wardens who had experience with them. And if they were indeed pleased with Adams's service and products, they would send them in his direction. Further, existing clients provided "showrooms" where he could invite prospective customers to see an actual installation for themselves. On February 10, 1912, for example, Adams wrote to Horace E. Flack of Maryland's Department of Legislative Reference (who was another Osborne referral), inviting him to Trenton, where "I could

A brass plate used by the Adams Electric Company on its installations, also in the collection of Adams Electric Company materials at Rutgers University's Special Collections and University Archives. *Carl F. Adams Papers, Special Collections and University Archives, Rutgers University Libraries, Ac.2399. Picture by the author.*

then show you the Plant in all it's [*sic*] details and have a test prepared giving practically a reproduction of the actual work done by the machine."

Unfortunately for Adams, not every state contemplating electrocution always followed through. Flack responded how the representative who introduced the bill to switch over "seems to think that the bill will hardly become a law at the present session."

The shift from hanging to electrocution often came in the middle of a normal flow of jurisprudence that was still sentencing people to die irrespective of the methods to be employed. This placed a degree of stress on Carl Adams—and gives terrible literality to the term "deadline." For if Adams failed to deliver on his contract on time, it would do more than be bad for his business—it would also drag out the pending death of someone thus condemned and, with this, the very notion of "cruel and unusual." It was a pressure Adams evidently keenly felt and frequently passed along to vendors, with earnest entreaties to swiftness.

The most well-documented installation found in the Rutgers files is for South Carolina, showing the process from order to execution.

South Carolina

"We accept your propersition [*sic*] of April, 22d, 1912, and agree to pay you 40 per cent on the delivery at the S.C. Penitentiary of the Electric Chair and other necessary equipments and 40 per cent when installed and successfully tested and the balance 20 per cent after the first execution." Adams had a deadline of June 1, 1912, to complete the installation, pending an expected execution.

What he had proposed was:

> *Will furnish erected complete one electrocuting plant as follows—One electric chair with high tension platform; one switch board and one testing resistance box with iron doors; one special resistance box; one controlling rheostatic machine with iron enclosure; one testing lamp board; two head electrodes; two leg electrodes; two sets of sponges; one set of leather straps; duplicate line of high tension lead cables from switch board to service entrance with two double throw switches, distance within hundred foot; one high tension floor box and mast arm with electrode connections and lamp sockets; duplicate set of high tension porcelain fuse blocks and fuses. Supervision of first electrocution. Price Twenty Eight Hundred Dollars.*

He assured the South Carolina Penitentiary and the architects of its new "death house," Todd & Benson, "I use only the best of materials obtainable and the finest workmanship so there is no possible chance of a break down unless someone should deliberately damage it."

This was the start of a series of correspondence by Adams and his company with the various vendors for the parts he would need. He used many local Trenton suppliers. On May 12, 1912, for example, he sent a letter to the Trenton Pattern Works for wooden chair and platform, asking that it be made like the one it evidentially also made for his Virginia job. "The most important point is that you have it ready by June 1," he told the company. But he added, "I have contracted personally with the State of South Carolina for the installation of electric chair so as not to get into complications with the present troubles of the Adams Electric Company, therefore I will personally pay you for this work just as soon as you have it ready." He doesn't elaborate on the "present troubles," but if he was writing a personal check, it seems to hint at financial. But more on this later.

The Trenton Pattern Works replied that it would "quote...on the chair and platform of solid oak finished dark in natural wood and furnished with polished bronze trimmings...made in the very best manner with solid oak seat perforated but you to furnish all straps...for the sum of seventy five dollars." The straps would come from Joseph M. Middleton, whose letterhead advertises him as a "Manufacturer and Dealer in Harness, Horse Clothing, Robes, Trunks and Valises" at No. 8 North Warren Street, Trenton. In his order, dated May 16, 1912, Adams had Middleton supply:

> *2 ankle straps 3/16" x 20" long*
> *2 forearm 3/16" x 25"*
> *1 body 3/16" x 4' 6"*
> *1 chest strap 3/16" x 3' 6"*
> *1 head nose strap*

He ordered rubber parts from Joseph Stokes Rubber Co. and steel parts from Barbour Bros. Iron and Steel, both of Trenton. Additionally, there were a number of details in an electric chair setup that needed to be attended to. He ordered six square yards of one-fourth-inch-thick "Corrugated Rubber Matting for use around switchboard" from the New Jersey Cloth Company of Trenton (and with offices in New York, Chicago, St. Louis, Pittsburgh and Washington, D.C.). That would have been to provide insulation for the operator. Horace E. Fine Company, General Engravers, at 19 East State Street, Trenton, was hired to engrave the labels on the plates for the switchboard.

He seems to have used local sources where possible, but the apparatus was created out of parts from a variety of vendors in the Northeast. In the case of the insulated cables, he asked for quotes from the National India Rubber Company of Church Street, New York City, and B. Latham & Company of Broadway and Murray Street, New York City, as well as from the old Trenton industrialists John A. Roebling's Sons Co. For many of the electrical components, he turned to Keystone Electrical Instrument Company over in Philadelphia. American Transformer Company, 153 Miller Street, Newark, supplied the transformers; a dozen condensers came from Bausch & Lomb Optical Co., Rochester, New York; and the Macallen Company of Boston supplied "insulated joints."

Two vendors in particular, however, had him nervous about making his deadline. He had ordered multiple parts from Westinghouse Electric & Manufacturing Company: a 3,450-volt primary, 2,000-volt secondary, forty-cycle, single-phase, Type S transformer for $185; a type D oil switch, double pole, double throw; two type D oil switches; four plug switches, mountings and faceplates; type S lightning arresters for 3,500 volts AC, etc. When it came to how he was going to pay for all this, Adams was very particular:

Regarding the payment for this material if you will send me your invoice for same by return mail I will forward you my certified check in payment for same at once, with the distinct understanding, however, that said check is not to be used until you are ready to make delivery of the material, said delivery to be positively made within the time agreed upon between ourselves.

A Mr. Lyon of Westinghouse's Detail & Supply Division wrote back that he had "taken the matter of credit up a little further and we regret to advise that we will be unable to accept your order without cash in full for same or certified check. We are bringing this matter to your attention so that no delay will occur should you feel in need of the apparatus upon which we quoted you while in the office."

Two days later, he sent them a check, "with the distinct understanding that it is not to be deposited until you send shipping memo for the above material." These were critical parts that would hold up construction, and Adams's frustration shows through when he added, "Now will you please ship this material immediately so that there is no further delay."

Adams had sent a check for $97.74—he had built in his own 5 percent discount for payment up front. Evidently, Westinghouse never agreed to that. One can imagine Adams's annoyance when he received his check back with the letter stating, "We regret that we are unable to accept your check insofar as you have deducted 5% for spot cash, also with the restriction in not allowing us to deposit same at the time of entering order...we can only enter this order upon receipt of certified check covering full amount of $104.68 without any restrictions."

Indeed, Adams comes across in his letters as somewhat dictatorial—he *tells* rather than *asks*. Whether he just assumed Westinghouse would extend to him what he considered a standard business practice or was trying to slip one by is uncertain. But he was obviously frustrated with how it was handled, writing back:

I trust that you did not delay getting out this material while all the writing was taking place, as you know how important it is for me to have this material, therefore please follow the matter up immediately and get it down to me without any further delay...As to placing the restrictions on using of the check, this was simply done at the time for the purpose of having you make a special effort to get the shipping bill for me at the quickest possible time. As far as the checks are concerned, if it is any help at all to the Westinghouse Co. to use the money before shipping the stuff I have no objection whatsoever to your making use of the money...It also seems rather peculiar way of doing business to return a certified check. Why didn't you keep it and have us send you an additional check. I suppose, though, that you fellows have to do everything just so according to red tape otherwise you cannot do any business. Now please, Mr. Lyon, as a personal favor to me, see that I get this material at once.

This exchange took place in May 1912—far too close for comfort for an apparent June 1 deadline. When, by June 4, he still did not have the items from Westinghouse, he wrote, "Now, it is of the utmost importance that I receive this material at once and I would request that you follow this matter up at once and see that this material is forwarded without further delay. It has delayed the job considerably now and is causing considerable annoyance by the delay."

How firm that June 1 deadline really was is suspect. Adams seems to have built in extra time before the first execution—and it was a good thing. Parts were out of stock, and Westinghouse sent what it could piecemeal together. When they arrived, some were broken, and Adams wrote back as late as June 26 that replacements had to be shipped.

The classic image of an electrocution involves the dramatic "throwing of the switch." In fact, there was no such switch with Adams's installations. A rheostat was dialed up, increasing the current. Getting that critical piece of equipment, however, proved an additional headache for Adams. On May 21, 1912, Ward Leonard Electric Co. of Bronxville, New York, informed him, "Please note that we cannot make up the variable electrocution rheostat in the time allowed—that is, we cannot make delivery of the complete machine by June 1st, but we can supply the resistance units complete with mounting rods and segments."

In other words, while it couldn't send a complete unit, it could send all the parts and diagrams so Adams's electricians could assemble it themselves. Adams received the parts but not the diagram that would show how to assemble it all. "In further reference to this matter," Adams wrote back when he got the parts, he "wish[ed] to state that your Mr. Waller and Mr. Kemp both promised that you would send me the shop drawing of the variable rheostat and also a chart of the units according to their steps so that I can give to my shop man to assist him in the assembling of these units." He remained also in need of another small but critical detail—a brass faceplate with arrows showing which way to turn the knob "to raise and lower voltage."

It wasn't until June 7 that Ward sent him a "complete drilling template and wiring diagram for your electrocution rheostat," with the suggestion that he lay the bits and pieces out first to make sure everything will fit properly before actually drilling.

Part of the problem was that while Ward had done the rheostat for the Trenton job, it couldn't find the template and had to re-create it. Aside from noting that several tubes had been broken in shipping or were missing from the order, Adams informed Ward, "I also wish to let you know that your sketch is not just right but I'll excuse you for getting it wrong, as it is a hard lay-out." He could afford, perhaps, to be charitable since his men discovered the mistakes beforehand by comparing it to the template they had for Trenton.

Still, the delay caused by the broken and missing parts was vexing: "Please do not delay the sending of the units as I have everything ready to ship now and just need these few tubes to complete both the Test Resistance and the Variable Rheostat. I want to ship the outfit by next Tuesday's steamer so will you be so good as to send these tubes by express at once so that I won't be held up." Ward sent the needed parts at no charge.

He wrote to Ward on June 21 but had evidently begun shipping some of the equipment earlier. Records show materials being sent via the Trenton Transportation Company to Philadelphia on June 10 and then on to Columbia, South Carolina, on the Seaboard Air Line Railway. Given this was 1912, "Air Line" was a descriptive rather than literal term. By July 1, Ward informed Adams that "shipment arrived at Columbia, S.C. morning of June 17th, consignees did not take delivery of same until the 24th. The reason that the Penitentiary people did not accept delivery before that date, was on account of them not being prepared to install same at the time of arrival."

Clearly, June 1 had been a self-imposed deadline, given that the client wasn't ready to begin actual installation until near the end of July. Adams always had men on-site to supervise not only the installation but also the training of staff in the use of the contraption. And he would always be on hand to witness the first execution in his chair.

While Adams appears to have designed much of the equipment himself (probably based on what he had learned from Edison or observed at Sing Sing), he did find at least one improvement thanks to an independent inventor. N.K. White, of Virginia, had sent him a diagram of a new and improved electrode he had developed, to which Adams replied in a February 10, 1910 letter, "Your scheme is first-class and is no doubt a big improvement over the electrodes which we furnished with our chair equipment. Ever since we had the accident with the leg electrode at your first execution [in Virginia] when the strap broke off I have been experimenting with some different things."

By the time Adams was making the chair for South Carolina, White had patented his design, and Adams agreed to use it, paying seventy-five dollars for the rights and suggesting he might want to buy the patent outright for future use. White liked that idea and offered that if he did, he wouldn't charge Adams for using his electrodes on the South Carolina chair. But Adams demurred in a June 25, 1912 letter, "Now Captain I will not allow this generosity; this has nothing to do with the future business and I shall send you a check for $75.00 as agreed as soon as I get my first payment from Columbia [South Carolina]."

Hard Times?

Success continued to attract customers, though it didn't always pan out. In April 1913, a year following South Carolina, The B-R Electric & Telephone Mfg. Co. of Kansas City, Missouri, wrote to Adams. It had been contracted to install an electrocution system for "one of the Western Panitentiaries [*sic*]" and wanted to get the equipment from him. The catch was that it wanted to be the one to perform the actual installation. Adams's reply demonstrates how confident he was in his own performance by that point:

> *Replying I would say that I sell my equipment only direct and install it myself on account of giving an absolute guarantee with each outfit that I build...I also wish to mention that my Electrocuting Apparatus is fully protected and is today the only equipment in use that can be operated from an exterior source of power supply such as is furnished by electrical light or power companies...I devoted a great deal of time and study to the designing of this apparatus realizing that for the work which it is intended the machine must be absolutely sure in its work, safe in its handling, and positively fool-proof. That I have succeeded in these points is demonstrated by the successful operation of the several Plants in use in the various States.*

In the end, he would turn down the contract. But this demonstrates that there were competitors out for the business in an admittedly shrinking market that was never all that large to begin with. Back in 1910, when he was corresponding with White about his patent, Adams enquired if White had heard anything about the state of the electric chair in North Carolina, since Virginia was closer than New Jersey. A local competitor had beaten him out on the contract, and he was annoyed that it had not returned the photographs he sent with his proposal. But more than loss of business, it seemed to justify his self-pride: "From newspaper reports I found that they are still trying to get the outfit to work and that one of the criminals has already had five respites and the chair is still inoperative."

It is difficult to say how successful Adams really was with all this. Based on the balance of enquiries and shipping information in the Rutgers collection, it would appear that he lost as many contracts as he won. Perhaps the most interesting solicitation came from outside the United States.

In January 1913, the Colonial Stores, identified on its letterhead as "Purveyors and Provision Suppliers, Canton, China," wrote to the warden of Virginia's State Penitentiary in Richmond:

> *We have written to the firm of Montgomery Ward & Co. Chicago for information regarding an apparatus for executing criminals by electricity, same as those used in some of the states of America. They have referred us to write you for information regarding this machine. We have a customer an [sic] high official in Canton who wishes to adopt the same method for this part of the country…I will be ever so thankful for your kind assistance. Wishing you greater prosperity in 1913 than you have ever had before, I remain yours sincerely, J.A. Cheong, Manager."*

The only thing odder than writing to Montgomery Ward for an electric chair was that the question came from a company that also specialized in "canned goods, dried fruits, wines, spirits, tobaccos and cigars."

Adams replied, "The price for this machine will be cash $3000.00, delivered on board ship at New York." Added to that would be the costs for man to go to oversee installations at five dollars a day while in transit and then ten dollars a day during the actual work. He estimated that it would all take a month from the receipt of the order to ship and then another two weeks to install. There were, of course, technical questions about the electrical systems overseas:

> *It will be necessary to receive current delivered from an exterior source. In the United States here this current is furnished by the Light and Power*

Companies and is Alternating Current of not less than 2200 volts; it is immaterial to us how much higher the voltage may be and whether it is one, two, or three phase, or what the cycle ratio may be, as all we need to know from you when ordering the machine is what the primary line voltage is, what the cycle is, and what the phase is, and then we will build the machine to suit your current conditions...Should you decide to purchase one of these machines for your Government you will be restricted from placing a higher price on this machine than what is a legitimate profit in consistency with your business. And I reserve the right to pass upon this price before the offer is made. Ordinarily a profit of 20 to 25% should be sufficient for you to handle the proposition.

As there is no paperwork indicating an order in the collection, it may be that this job never came about—nor did ones in Arkansas, Kentucky or Maryland. But there are other clearer clues as to financial troubles. Adams declared bankruptcy in 1900; he was dealing personally with suppliers on the South Carolina order, and a May 21, 1913 letter asking the status of the Arkansas death penalty law was from an A. Lee Grover, identified on the letterhead as a "successor" to Adams Electric Company.

Even before that, Adams seemed to be playing a game—he would order parts, and vendors would invoice Adams Electrical Company, but he would write back, saying it was really ordered by A. Lee Grover and that if they would resubmit the bill to that name, it would be paid immediately. While it isn't completely clear, this has the appearance of being a stalling tactic to delay having to pay the bill.

Cars and Blue Laws

Obviously, electric chairs weren't Adams's sole business. He seems to have been involved with another new marvel of the modern age: the automobile. According to a column, "Among the Automobilists" in the January 1, 1909 *Trenton Evening Times*, H.A. Anderson, an automaker from Detroit, had sold out all his stock at a New York car show and had to order his factory to make more for an upcoming show in Chicago. That it was the first time he had had such a success was noteworthy for him, but for history it is worth noting that he was selling electric cars—one hundred years before it again became popular.

And among the agents he assured he would still fill orders for was Adams in Trenton.

In February, Adams listed for sale a 1906 Ford touring car "in first class condition" for $375. Evidently, Adams picked up extra money renting out garage space. The "Automobiles and Automobilists" column—something of a social column for automobile owners—in the April 17, 1909 *Trenton Evening Times* mentioned, "The Adams garage is storing Dr. Charles P. Britton's new Premier touring car" and seemed to consider it newsworthy that "The Adams Electrical Company's garage recently installed twenty-four lockers." Further, E.H. Savage received his new Regal, Model A, thirty-horsepower touring car from Adams Electrical Company, and David S. Swift, local taxicab manager, was having four cars "cared for by the Adams Electrical Company."

Adams was also a family man. He and his wife, Catherine H. Aller Adams, had a son, two daughters and eight grandchildren. And he was active in local community affairs around Trenton. At the same time he was responding to solicitations for electric chairs from China, his company also did the "electrical effects" at the Mohawk Canoe Club's "George Washington dance" and was a founding member and historian for the Trenton Tadpoles Club.

While he obviously had no moral compunction to capital punishment, he was of a different mind when it came to watching a motion picture show on the Sabbath. So-called blue laws in Trenton outlawed movie theaters being open on Sundays. Given that for most of the working-class folks who were their most likely patrons, Sunday was their only day off, this was a threat to their livelihoods. So on August 28, 1921—a Sunday—they all agreed to remain open in defiance of the law. It was a lucrative protest—some eighteen thousand tickets were said to have been sold.

The Interchurch Federation League, however, saw this open defiance as nothing less than a war on religion. Leading the resistance was state Quartermaster General C. Edward Murray. Among those who reminded Trentonians of the Fourth Commandment—Remember the Sabbath day, to keep it holy—was the Reverend John H. Fox at St. Mary's Cathedral, the same Reverend Fox whose Silver Jubilee Adams's company had helped to celebrate in 1905 with electric light shows.

Trenton's public safety commissioner, George LaBarre, begged to disagree, not seeing it as something the city ought to get involved in. He instructed the chief of police to leave unmolested any theater-owner open on a Sunday by virtue of a technicality—the law specifically forbade "dancing" and "fiddling," neither of which tended to go on in a movie house.

General Murray was furious—if the city's officials would not enforce the law, his "police" would. He had Sheriff Walter Firth on his side, and they handed out deputy's badges to some sixty-five members of the Interchurch Federation League—including Carl F. Adams. They would bust the movie theaters that were open, arresting the owners and sending the disappointed sinning patrons home.

Trial of the Century

In 1932, New Jersey and the nation—indeed the world—were gripped by the tragic kidnapping and murder of transatlantic hero Charles A. Lindbergh's son, Charles Jr. The boyish Lindbergh had captured imaginations with his historic first solo airplane flight across the Atlantic Ocean in 1927. Given his heroic status, the public was more acutely aghast when his and Ann Morrow Lindbergh's eighteen-month-old son went missing and was then found dead near their East Amwell, New Jersey home. When, two years later, German

immigrant Bruno Richard Hauptmann was arrested and charged with the crime, he was considered the "Most Hated Man in the World." From January 2 to February 13, 1935, Hauptmann was put on trial—the "Trial of the Century," according to the media. Throughout, he vehemently protested that he was innocent, and the case remains one that is questioned and rehashed by historians. But in the end, he was convicted and sentenced to die in the electric chair.

The electric chair at the New Jersey State Prison as it appeared around the time of Bruno Hauptmann's execution in 1936. *New Jersey State Archives, Department of State.*

In Charles Adams's electric chair.

At the time, a newspaper sought out the man who built the instrument that would end the life of that "Most Hated Man in the World." The copy in the Rutgers collection is unidentified but described how "[t]he impending execution of Bruno Richard Hauptmann means little to the man who built the electric chair for the New Jersey State Prison." He was described as "a middle-aged electrician, living at 1122 Riverside Avenue, [and as] a man of ponderous reserve good nerves and calm temper of mind...[The chair] worked perfectly the first time on the night of December 11, 1907, and is as good as new now after 116 executions. That, he feels, is something."

The End of Capital Punishment in New Jersey

New Jersey held capital punishment laws on the books until a moratorium imposed by the U.S. Supreme Court in 1972. In *Furman v. Georgia*, by a five-to-four decision, the court considered it cruel and unusual punishment and, therefore, unconstitutional. Justices William Brennan Jr. (born in Newark, New Jersey) and Thurgood Marshall both considered the practice unconstitutional in all cases, while others had a problem with how it was being handed out on the state level, pointing to arbitrariness and racial bias. Guidelines were imposed, and the states were told to revise their sentencing processes accordingly. When capital convictions occurred in Georgia, Florida, Texas, North Carolina and Louisiana, they were appealed to the U.S. Supreme Court with a view to abolish the death penalty once and for all on the grounds of being fundamentally cruel and unusual. Consolidated with *Gregg v. Georgia* in 1976, the court instead upheld the penalty so long as certain broad guidelines were adopted by the state legislatures into their capital sentencing processes. These were designed to remove some of the discretion that led to abuse, permit appellate review and allow the judge or jury to take the character and record of the defendant into account. As far as Justice Potter Stewart was concerned, the death penalty was "cruel and unusual in the same way that being struck by lightning is cruel and unusual."

New Jersey's last execution took place in 1963, when Ralph Hudson died in Adams's electric chair for stabbing his estranged wife to death. The post–*Gregg v. Georgia* period is called the "modern era" of capital punishment, and in 2007, New Jersey became the first state to abolish the death penalty completely.

Pro– and anti–capital punishment groups still debate the merits, morals and even the economics of the practice in other states and around the world.

Conclusion

Death came for Carl F. Adams at age seventy-eight on October 13, 1946, after an illness that confined him to Mercer Hospital. Regardless of whatever else he had done in his life, he was still identified first and foremost in his obituary as the state's "Death Chair Builder." It seems he probably wouldn't have minded the distinction. As of then, his creation had successfully taken the lives of 134 men.

His chair from Trenton now sits in the New Jersey State Police Museum, the product of a controversial and macabre twist to Trenton's industrial heritage.

Chapter 4

WILDWOOD

WHERE ROCK FIRST ROLLED

Rock 'n' roll was an evolutionary process—we just looked around and it was here." So wrote the singer and music historian Billy Vera. Like all evolutions, "firsts" are relative and impossible to pin down as anything like a single, fixed wellspring. A rough approximation is that what we now recognize as rock-and-roll emerged from a culture clash between white country-western and black rhythm and blues—earthy, soulful and basic but infectious rhythms that shimmied and shook their way out of the rough-hewn vernacular landscapes of front porches and juke joints and into the ears of a generation seeking a soundtrack all its own.

Even the alliterative phrase rock-and-roll itself has a longer and more complicated heritage than most people realize. Sailors in the seventeenth century were among the first to stitch the words together to describe the back-and-forth motions of their ships—rocking was forward and backward, and rolling was side to side. And it pops up in everything from nineteenth-century hymns describing the physical motions of the raptured to code in secular folk music as a euphemism for sex. That latter connotation was more applicable to the birth of rock-and-roll music, describing the suggestive dancing by which youths scandalized their elders.

Nevertheless, where historians may revel in this murky complexity, we still like the idea of "firsts"—some tangible touchstone of where it all began. The first time rock-and-roll was employed as a name for the musical form is generally credited to the Cleveland disc jockey Alan Freed in 1951 on WJW—850 on your AM dial.

It should be possible, too, to identify when this bastard hybrid emerged as a distinct cultural, as well as musical, form. And, many maintain, it first entered the ears of the public in a South Jersey club.

Crazy Man, Crazy

It could be said that rock-and-roll started with something sounding like a riddle: why did the country-western yodeler cross the road? During the summer of 1951, a country band called the Saddlemen was appearing at Wildwood's HofBrau Club. Across the street, at the Rip Tide, was playing a rhythm and blues band called the Treniers. Between sets or on nights off, it wasn't uncommon for musicians to go check out whoever happened to be playing at nearby clubs. So the country crooner strolled across the street from his hotel—and was blown away by the other band's raucous sound.

Listening to them side-by-side now, it isn't difficult to hear how Bill Haley's hillbilly boogie shares stylistic sensibilities with Milt Trenier's swinging jive. At the time, however, it wasn't quite so intuitive. More than a street stood between them. Musicians had crossed color boundaries before, and music industry executives were beginning to appreciate the financial rewards this seemed to promise. But it wasn't all that long before—1949, in fact—that *Billboard* magazine dropped the term "race records" for its black music charts in favor of "rhythm and blues." Many white parents, however, would still fret over their children dancing the night away to "that jungle music."

Not that any of that got in the way of Haley sharing a song he wrote with Trenier, "Rock-a-Beatin' Boogie." It had been first recorded by the Esquire Boys in 1952, and the Treniers went on to release it as a single in 1954. The cross-pollination had begun—not for the first time, but this time it would certainly bear amazing fruit.

The influence of exposure to rhythm and blues in the clubs of Wildwood and elsewhere had inspired a shift in Haley's sound away from strict country western and toward this novel hybrid. He called his new act Bill Haley & His Comets—referencing Halley's Comet—and they debuted Labor Day weekend of 1952. The following April, they recorded "Crazy Man, Crazy."

Historians tend to agree that "Crazy Man, Crazy" was the first fully formed example of the rock-and-roll genre. Stylistically, it was a true hybrid, between the "go, go, go everybody" call reminiscent of jump blues

Bill Haley (right) and his Comets during a TV appearance with Joey D'Ambrosio and Dick Richards.

and a short lap steel guitar solo adding a mild dash of country. It definitely staked rock-and-roll's claim on the music scene as a legitimate style. It was even included in the soundtrack for a live 1953 television broadcast of "Glory in the Flower" for the CBS anthology series *Omnibus*. The production was notable for including another eventual icon of the 1950s: James Dean.

But in terms of cultural impact, it is difficult to argue that "Crazy Man, Crazy" was the start of the rock-and-roll revolution, its priority notwithstanding. It peaked for only a week at number twelve in June 1953 on *Billboard* and did marginally better on the *Cashbox* chart, spending two weeks at number eleven. The true breakout song that would firmly establish rock-and-roll—and Bill Haley—in American culture was yet to come.

"Rock Around the Clock"

Pop music had given songwriters and music orchestrators a new way of making a quick buck. A lot of it wasn't technically sophisticated in terms of lyrics or structure, and much just copped the long-established twelve-bar blues format. But if it was catchy enough to be danced to, it could earn its creator royalties through such respected industry unions as ASCAP (the American Society of Composers, Authors and Publishers).

Max C. Freedman, a songwriter from Pennsylvania with a minor hit called "Sioux City Sue" (co-written with Dick Thomas in 1945) was one of them. Sometime around 1952, he had come up with the words for what amounted to a novelty song. The tune was supplied by James E. Myers, under the pseudonym Jimmy DeKnight. There is some question of whether he contributed to the lyrics at all, but the result was titled, "We're Gonna Rock Around the Clock Tonight!"

Max C. Freedman (right) with Dick Thomas in a 1946 promotional photo for their minor hit, "Sioux City Sue."

A tad unwieldy, the name would get trimmed to "(We're Gonna) Rock Around the Clock" and finally "Rock Around the Clock." Before it would become really famous, it was first recorded on March 20, 1954, by Sonny Dae and His Knights, an Italian-American novelty band that gave it a jazzy bounce. James Myers would later insist, however, that the song had really been written with Bill Haley in mind. Haley had been playing it at his live shows since 1953, and the only reason he hadn't recorded it was a personal grudge. Haley was signed with Essex Records, whose head, Dave Miller, personally detested Myers and vowed that no song by him would ever be issued under the Essex label.

When Haley switched to the Decca recording company in 1954, he could finally record the song he had been playing on stage for a year already. Like Dae's version, it at first achieved only a modest, local success. But by July 1955, it had shot up to number one on the *Billboard* charts and would stay there for eight solid weeks. It spent seven weeks topping *Cashbox* and UK pop charts. The tremendous success of "Rock Around the Clock," more than any other song, opened the sonic floodgates of making rock-and-roll mainstream to youth culture throughout the United States and even around the world.

So, as "firsts" go, "Rock Around the Clock" was, technically speaking, second. But in terms of changing history, most music historians consider it *the* song where the rock revolution began. The delay in Haley's recording it, however, meant that the fuse had been smoldering for nearly a year. Comets bass player Marshall Lytle and drummer Dick Richards related how they first performed the song before an audience at a joint called Phil and Eddie's

Surf Club. Fittingly, the club was located where Haley had first started soaking in the inspirations that led to his artistic shift: Wildwood, New Jersey.

Twisting on *Bandstand*

Regardless of how one wants to define rock-and-roll's "first"—or if it really matters—Wildwood was definitely one of the laboratories where the early experiments were done. It had already been a place where, during the big band era of the 1940s and early '50s, the Convention Hall and Hunt's Starlight Ballroom hosted such legends of the day as Vaughn Monroe, Woody Herman and Charlie Spivak. Some sixty million listeners tuned in to hear Tex Beneke and his orchestra broadcasting live from the Starlight.

When record companies and DJs saw the girls swooning over Frank Sinatra in the late 1940s, they understood just how ripe the teen pop market was for picking. Philadelphia disc jockey Bob Horn took his popular television

Philadelphia may claim to be the home of Dick Clark's *American Bandstand*, but the show first gained national attention broadcasting from Wildwood, New Jersey, in 1957.

Bandstand program to Wildwood for the summer in the mid-1950s, broadcasting live from the Starlight but spinning records instead of having a live band. The people dancing and having a good time brought the party into viewers' living rooms six times a week, often capturing as much as 60 percent of the daytime audience, making Horn a wealthy man indeed. Fate intervened in an unfortunate way on July 9, 1956, when Horn was fired after being convicted of drunk driving (he was acquitted of a statutory rape charge). His replacement was Dick Clark, and the show was re-christened *American Bandstand.*

Clark and *American Bandstand* would legitimize rock-and-roll and youth culture as an industry, often against the protestations of their parents' generation. But at first, Clark and his show were a strictly local phenomenon, not known beyond the environs of Philadelphia. All that changed on August 5, 1957, when *American Bandstand* was broadcast live on ABC-TV, from the Starlight Ballroom in Wildwood, New Jersey. Within a year, he was a star—and had outgrown Wildwood. Nevertheless, with the teen "bandstand" concept established, even without Clark, the Starlight was able to enjoy continued success from "record hops."

These days, the dances seem quite tame, but in 1960, one in particular was considered scandalously provocative. The dance craze known as the Twist, involved moves the more conservative folks saw as downright salacious—so, naturally, the kids loved to do it. The inspiration came out of the song by the same name with a curious pedigree. The word "twist" had a double meaning at least as far back at 1938, when Jelly Roll Morton sang "Mama, mama, look at sis, she's out on the levee doing the double twist" in "Winin' Boy Blues." Sure, it was a description of dancing but also of sex.

Hank Ballard's guitar player, Cal Green, had heard a song by that name from Brother Joe Wallace. The problem was that Wallace was in the Sensational Nightingales, a gospel group that could never record lyrics with such a double meaning. So, without such compunctions, Ballard and Green adapted a song originally called "Is Your Love for Real" into the simpler "The Twist." They recorded it as a B side in 1958 with the ballad "Teardrops on Your Letter," written by King Records' producer Henry Glover, on the A side. Glover and Ballard bet on whose song would be the hit. Ballard, of course, would win that bet, but not in the way he probably thought.

Dick Clark played Ballard's version on *American Bandstand* on the recommendation of a Baltimore DJ, Buddy Dean, who had a similar program. When it proved popular, Clark sought to book Ballard to perform it live, but when he was unavailable, he hired a local singer by the name of Chubby Checker. Between 1960 and 1962, Checker made "The Twist" his own, topping the *Billboard* Hot 100 for both 1961 and 1962.

In the meantime, a silver Jaguar XKE pulled up to Wildwood's Rainbow Club, out of which strolled Chubby Checker, intending to add a little pizazz to the live version of his hit that night. Rather than just sing, he started swiveling his hips and shoulders, bending his knees, shifting from foot to foot—*twisting* in time to the music. The kids in the audience followed suit, and so was born the dance craze that would thrill the teenagers and shock their parents—another rock-and-roll "first" right there in Wildwood.

Doo-Wop

Few places in America would come to fully embody the era of the 1950s like Wildwood—and not just as a fertile ground for the germination of rock-and-roll.

Like most coastal areas, the economic life of the Jersey Shore came to revolve around either maritime industries or tourism. Nearby Cape May's Victorian-styled bed-and-breakfasts and hotels had long provided a genteel spot to catch the ocean breezes, and Long Branch had hosted presidents and dignitaries. Ocean Grove was founded as a Christian camp-meeting resort. Other towns added amusement piers with rides and swimming to attract families from New Jersey and nearby Philadelphia.

American car culture boomed in the postwar years, drawing thousands of motorist families, couples and teenagers from New Jersey and nearby Philadelphia to partake of Wildwood's combination of family fun and rocking nightlife—and they all needed a place to stay. Wildwood would come to pack more motels per square mile than anywhere else, leading to a frenzy of creativity among their owners to stand out. Structurally, most motels followed the same few basic L and U shapes. Where they differentiated themselves was with fancifully themed façades and flashy neon signs. Plastic palm trees and faux-thatch turned a boring dime-a-dozen motel into a Polynesian paradise; sweeping curves and angles evoked the hipness of the brave new atomic and space age; electric coach-lights, functionless copulas and split-rail fences were tacked on to a patriotic red, white and blue "Phony Colony" theme; and so on.

Technically, the term "doo-wop" refers to a vocally driven rhythm and blues style that's different from the more instrument-driven rock-and-roll. Yet it has evolved to encompass not only the distinct 1950s music styles but also the concurrent over-the-top architectural style of Wildwood.

These days, Wildwood has a conflicted relationship with its doo-wop identity. On the one hand, the exuberantly tacky motels are what differentiated the city from the nearby more genteel Cape May or the pious roots of Ocean Grove. Indeed, where Ocean Grove, founded as a Christian camp-meeting resort, is called "God's Square Mile at the Jersey Shore," booking agents in the 1950s dubbed Wildwood "Little Las Vegas." On the other hand, some residents are sick of doo-wop—it's a passé style, and progress lies not in tacky little motels but in multistory, vinyl siding-clad condos and rentals, even if it means losing a uniqueness some no longer care about.

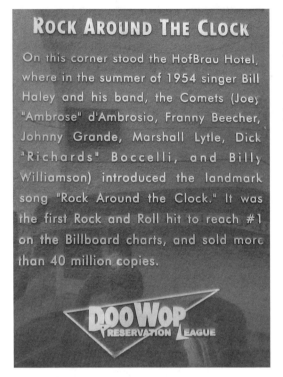

ROCK AROUND THE CLOCK

On this corner stood the HofBrau Hotel, where in the summer of 1954 singer Bill Haley and his band, the Comets (Joey "Ambrose" d'Ambrosio, Franny Beecher, Johnny Grande, Marshall Lytle, Dick "Richards" Boccelli, and Billy Williamson) introduced the landmark song "Rock Around the Clock." It was the first Rock and Roll hit to reach #1 on the Billboard charts, and sold more than 40 million copies.

The HofBrau is no more, but Wildwood remembers with this plaque in 2004. *Michael Hirsch.*

Every season, Wildwood seems to greet the summer with a handful fewer of the motels that made it famous. But some see that storied past not as something to run from but as something to be embraced as an economic engine again. There are efforts to get a historic district on the state and national Register of Historic Places comprising the surviving motel neighborhoods. The city has created a "How to Doo-Wop" guide for businesses that want to adopt the style. Some recent constructions include design elements of a sort of neo doo-wop.

Wildwood takes some civic pride in having been the setting for rock-and-roll's early developments. On October 16, 2004, five surviving members of the original Comets—Billy Williamson, Al Rex, Johnny Grande, Ralph Jones and Franny Beecher (Rudy Pompilli passed away in 1976 and Bill Haley in 1981)—gathered on the corner of Oak and Atlantic. They were there to unveil a historic marker on the site where they had taken the stage and unleashed on the world a sound that echoes and resonates to this day.

Chapter 5

BALLOONOMANIA DROPS IN ON DEPTFORD

W e live in an age today when the sight of an aircraft traversing the wild blue yonder is no big deal—and being *on* one is so routine as to be regarded more as a hassle than with a sense of wonder. Yet, of course, it wasn't all that long ago when seeing anything but birds aloft amongst the clouds was positively mind-blowing. In the early days of practical powered flight, airfields dotted the landscape, and Newark's airport established flying as an industry. But South Jersey played a role in an earlier form of manned flight—when the first hot-air balloon in North America lifted off into a crisp January sky.

Balloons

Once we humans mastered the ability of controlling fires, we would have noticed how embers shot skyward from our campfires. Hot air, being less dense, rises, so anything lightweight enough over the heat of a fire would be caught in the resulting upward drafts. At some point, someone would have the bright idea of letting go of a bag-like enclosure, mouth-down, over the fire and watching as it took off into the air. Paper is an intuitive choice of material, and given how the Chinese perfected some of the earliest examples of paper, it is no surprise they are credited with the first hot-air balloons.

Though they may have been used before, the earliest surviving records describe the *Kongming* lanterns, or sky lanterns, between AD 220 and 280. These were made of rice paper on a bamboo frame with a candle in the base. As the flame heated the air inside the lantern, the density dropped, and the whole thing, candle and all, lifted off into the sky. They were used on the battlefield to send signals, but they also found a role in celebrating festivals and are still used in China, Taiwan and Thailand. Not everyone, though, is happy that the tradition survives. Farmers lament crops lost to fires started by wayward lanterns, and apparently livestock have a habit of eating the remains of spent ones, making

The Chinese are credited with the *Kongming* sky lanterns, an early form of hot-air balloon.

them sick. There are companies specializing in more environmentally friendly versions—fire-resistant and biodegradable—but the Chinese city of Sanya still banned them, lest they interfere with aircraft.

Some scholars speculate that really big lanterns were built in order to carry observers high enough to spy on distant enemies—somehow the exigencies of war always end up driving innovation. If that were true, it would have been the first sustained manned flight. Others see evidence of such flight on the other side of the world, albeit still a somewhat controversial idea. The famed Nazca Lines geoglyphs—huge drawings and remarkably long and accurately straight lines etched into the surface of the deserts of Peru—can only really be fully appreciated from above, leading to a number of fringe "ancient alien" theories. But if the Nazca people, who created them between AD 400 and 650, had come up with hot-air balloon technology, invoking little green men would be unnecessary. It has been proven they could have done so with the resources available, but lacking any records of actually having done it, the idea of Nazca balloons remains only marginally more respectable than UFOs.

The first well-documented flight of a hot-air balloon in Europe was by Bartolomeu Lourenço de Gusmão, a Portuguese priest and naturalist born in the then colony of Brazil. On August 8, 1709, he traveled to Lisbon to demonstrate the idea before King John V, floating a spherical balloon to the

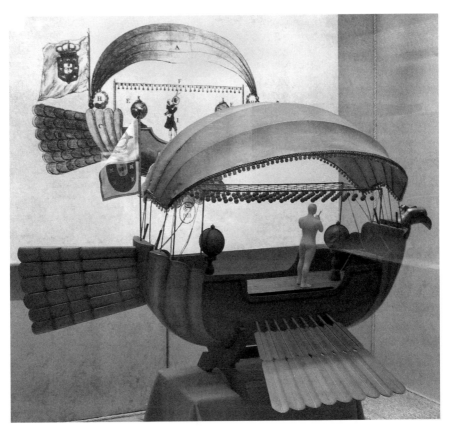

Bartolomeu Lourenço de Gusmão envisioned a fanciful manned airship capable of being steered but died before he could try building it. *Model at the Museo Aeronáutico y del Espacio.*

roof of the palace. The king was suitably enough impressed to give him a professorship and make him a canon. De Gusmão seems to have understood the potential of the technology, envisioning a fanciful controllable airship, but he died before he was able to experiment with actually building it.

It isn't known if anyone else tried making balloons big enough to carry people—but it's the kind of wonderfully crazy idea that *must* have fired the imaginations of more than a few dreamers. The first to turn the dream to reality—at least that we know of—were the French Montgolfier brothers, Joseph-Michel and Jacques-Etienne. After several unmanned experiments and a few using animals as unwitting test subjects, Jacques-Etienne launched himself on a balloon out of their workshop's backyard in Faubourg Saint-Antoine on October 15, 1783. Then their friend, Pilatre de Rozier, tried it

Left: Jacques-Etienne Montgolfier became the first-known human to be carried aloft in a tethered hot-air balloon in 1783.

Right: On November 21, 1783, Pilatre de Rozier (above) and the Marquis François d'Arlandes became the first humans known to have made an untethered balloon flight, traveling some five miles and reaching around three thousand feet in a Montgolfier balloon.

later that same day. Both rose eighty feet—we can say as much because that was the length of the tether that kept them attached to the ground.

The next month, however, they were ready to take their chances with free, *untethered* flying. They had the backing of King Louis XVI, who at first decreed expendable condemned prisoners would be used as passengers. Not wanting to let the honor of the first free flight go to some criminals, however, de Rozier and an army officer, Marquis François d'Arlandes, successfully petitioned the king to let them go instead. So, on November 21, 1783, they took off from the Château de la Muette outside western Paris, traveling a little over five miles and reaching an altitude of some three thousand feet. It could have gone father—four or five times as far, by some accounts—but the embers from the onboard fire kept catching the coated paper balloon on fire.

Nevertheless, the crowds were thrilled, and the idea—to embrace the admittedly obvious and painfully bad pun—really took off. A phenomenon

Jacques Alexander Cesar Charles took off in a hydrogen-filled balloon in 1783 in a flight witnessed by Benjamin Franklin. Alarmed peasants where he landed attacked the bizarre beast.

known as "balloonomania"—yes, that was the actual term used at the time—seized France and found its way across the Channel to England and elsewhere. Thrill-seekers sated adrenaline highs and won fame by public demonstrations before as many as hundreds of thousands of people who threatened riots if a display were delayed or called off. Images of balloons graced all manner of objects—ceramics, fans, hats, puffy clothing styles *au ballon*. There were even balloon-themed hairstyles.

Others, however, who hadn't caught the mania, were terrified by the appearance of floating spheres—especially if one landed in your fields and trampled your crops. Jacques Alexander Cesar Charles's hydrogen-filled balloon met an undignified end at such hands. He took off on August 27, 1783, before a large crowd—including Benjamin Franklin, who was in France at the time—but came down fifteen miles away in a field near the village of Genoesse, where the balloon was promptly attacked and destroyed by frightened peasants.

Like most technologies now viewed with hindsight as groundbreaking, ballooning was not without its naysayers, even amongst the more learned classes. The science-minded were curious about the physics involved, certainly. But of what *use* was this dangerous and unwieldy technology? The English poet, essayist, moralist, literary critic, biographer, editor and lexicographer Dr. Samuel Johnson wrote, "I know not that they [balloons] can possibly be of any use." Like powered aircraft in the early twentieth century, balloons were seen as amazing but still little more than mere novelties—outdoor parlor tricks to wow the masses.

As people debated the future utility of the balloon, there was still something deliciously enthralling about watching an "aeronaut" climb into the basket and fly off on the currents beneath the seemingly fragile sphere.

Jean-Pierre Blanchard

Among those caught up in the excitement was Jean-Pierre Blanchard (July 4, 1753–March 7, 1809; sometimes also known as Jean-Pierre François Blanchard). Just four months after the Montgolfier balloon first carried human passengers, Blanchard was launching his own hydrogen-filled balloon over the Champ de Mars, a park in Paris, on March 2, 1784. He took "oars" with him—wing-like surfaces on the end of poles with which he hoped to be able to push air around and maneuver the craft to some degree like a rowboat. His hopes at controlled flight were dashed, however—indeed, one might say "slashed"—by an irate spectator incensed by Blanchard's refusal to take him along. The man, Dupont de Chamon, was a student at École Militaire de Brienne—a military school where Napoleon was also going at the time—and drew his sword, slashing at the ropes that kept the thing moored and ruining Blanchard's oars. Blanchard had hoped to steer himself northeast, toward a landing in La Villete, but wound up at the mercy of the wind, which sent him first across the Seine River to the town of Billancourt and then back again to a landing in the middle of the street on the rue de Sèvres.

It was a clever and intuitive enough idea, but even if de Chamon's aggressive rudeness had not intervened, it is unlikely Blanchard's "rowing" would have made much difference to the outcome. But he didn't know that yet. When he moved to London in August 1784, he tried flapping wings and a windmill-like contraption on October 16, 1784—only the second balloon flight in England. Despite the failure of such creative means of propulsion, he still managed to make it over seventy-one miles from Chelsea to Sunbury and then on to Romsey.

A second flight, on November 30, 1784, included the interesting Dr. John Jeffries, a Boston-born Loyalist who had been a witness for the defense of British soldiers John Adams had idealistically argued following the Boston

Left: Jean-Pierre Blanchard. *U.S. Library of Congress.*

Right: In addition to his ballooning exploits, John Jeffries is credited as among the first people in America to keep long-range weather records. Wonderful Ballon Ascents, *Fulgence Marion, 1870.*

Massacre. As a doctor, Jeffries had treated the wounds of Patrick Carr, the last of the five Americans shot and killed that day. Jeffries went on to serve as a surgeon with the British army during the ensuing war, before moving to England until 1790. Despite his Loyalist sentiments, he was able to return to Boston and worked at a private practice until his death in 1819.

On January 7, 1785, Blanchard and Jeffries became the first to cross the English Channel in a hot-air balloon, floating between Dover Castle in England and Guînes, France, in about two and a half hours. The feat earned Blanchard a substantial pension granted by Louis XVI, but it had proven disappointing news for Jean-François Pilâtre de Rozier—the same aeronaut who shared the honor of the first (known) human flight in a balloon. He, along with Pierre Romain, had hoped to achieve the same first, from France to England, but was delayed by setbacks until overtaken by Blanchard and Jeffries. Gamely, they carried on, launching on June 15, 1785, but uncooperative winds blew them back over France. Somewhere near the coastal town of Wimereux, evidently the hydrogen balloon suddenly deflated, and the two men fell to their deaths, garnering the dubious honor of becoming the first balloon flight fatalities.

Blanchard went on to become the toast of Europe, touring his balloon demonstrations before cheering crowds and chalking up a string of first balloon flights in Belgium, Germany, the Netherlands and Poland. When the Holy Roman Emperor Leopold II was crowned king of Bohemia in Prague in September 1791, Blanchard's flight was a highlight of the coronation celebrations.

"In a word," Blanchard later wrote of his then-career forty-four flights, "I enjoyed a satisfaction which seemed to leave me nothing to wish for. I then thought of terminating my aerial excursions." He planned on retiring to a more quiet life, writing up his experiences and observations for the benefit of the public and scientific communities of Europe. Then, he described being seized by "an uneasy emotion."

America was still a novelty—a freshly formed new nation based on Enlightenment ideals of liberty that had managed to wrest itself from among the globe's most powerful empires (with, it is worth noting, French assistance). It was young and exciting. "The New World, so interesting by its situation," Blanchard explained, "offered to my emulation an attraction which I could not resist." America had yet to experience the thrill of the aeronaut, yet the "people who inhabit it appeared to me to be worthy of enjoying the sublime spectacle that it affords."

He enthused about America and Americans:

> *Ye People of America, ye wise and happy Nation, who knowing the full value of liberty, are not insensible to that of a just submission to the laws, you attract all my attention, and the desire of beholding you in the full enjoyment of the blessings of liberty, under the protection of your newly established government, fired my soul as much as the wish of acquiring some glory among you.*

On December 9, 1792, he landed by ship at Philadelphia, heaping even more flattering praise on the city, where he said, "I made it my duty, nay I was proud of attempting in this metropolis my first aerial ascent in America, and I derived from it the most sanguine expectations of a complete success." He was thrilled to be received by President George Washington—"the hero of liberty"—as well as Pennsylvania's governor, Thomas Mifflin.

He managed to secure use of Philadelphia's Walnut Street Prison as his launching site. This was the first multi-cell jail in the United States, and its walls offered protection for Blanchard's balloon and equipment against damage from the curious or even malicious public—he may have recalled the near-disaster of the de Chamon incident. But it would also provide a form of crowd control when it came to paying customers.

Blanchard's excursions were not without their expenses. Aside from the obvious travel and lodgings, there was the matter of transporting equipment. Balloons were not exactly off-the-shelf items to be found everywhere. His trip to America had been delayed by the necessity of procuring materials from London to Hamburg, where he was staying, and then shipping them across the Atlantic to Philadelphia. Aside from that, he needed to make his own hydrogen supply. The lighter-than-air quality of the gas had been known to chemists, and it wasn't long after the first flight of Montgolfier's hot-air balloon that it was realized the bag of the balloon could be filled instead with enough hydrogen to provide buoyancy. He may have been motivated by admiration for the new "wise and happy Nation," but this was also a moneymaking enterprise, and he had costs to cover.

"I soon gave notice to the public of my intention," he later described,

> *and immediately proposed a subscription for a sum which might lighten the burthen of my expenses...The day appointed for my experiment rose, one of the finest of the new year; I will also reckon it among the happiest of my life. It was presaged by a calm night, a serene sky, spangled with ten thousand glittering stars, whose light was eclipsed only by that of the returning sun.*

The morning dawned cold but overcast, but the sun burned off the haze "in such a manner that they appeared no more than cobwebs on the irradiated atmosphere."

President Washington was present to personally hand to Blanchard a letter to act as a sort of passport, instructing Americans to offer him "no hindrance or molestation" wherever he might land—not a bad idea given he spoke no English. "I never felt the value of glory so much as I did in that moment," gushed Blanchard, "in the presence of a Hero [*sic*]."

Aside from Washington, also on hand to witness the historic flight were John Adams, Thomas Jefferson, James Madison and James Monroe—all destined to be future presidents. Yet as star-struck as Blanchard might have been with Washington, as he ascended over Philadelphia, he was also struck by "the immense number of people which covered the open places, the roofs of houses, the steeples, the streets and the roads over which my flight carried me in the free space of the air." He would hold the scene as even more remarkable than "the pompous scenes of numerous assemblies" of highly ranked people to which he had become accustomed. There was something in the nature of a these free citizens shouting and saluting the United States and French flags he carried that meant more to him.

At about two hundred fathoms—a little over 365 feet—he felt the push of a stronger wind sending him over the Delaware River, where he startled a flock of wild pigeons. Over the river, he described how "the reflecting sunbeams painted to my eyes of a transparent white" and how the waterway appeared from that height to be a mere four inches wide.

Blanchard had with him a companion. "A little black dog, which a friend had entrusted me, seemed to feel sick at this height; he attempted several times to get out of the car [basket]; but finding no landing-place he took the prudent part to remain quietly beside me."

How this unwilling passenger came to be so "entrusted" was not explained, but sympathy elicited by the creature's displeased whining almost distracted Blanchard from contemplating the unique view they had of that little corner of America. "See here, I said to myself," he later waxed poetic, "this country for ever famous in history, by which philosophy as well as by dint of courage has acquired its liberty; its inhabitants preserve yet the primitive candor of the original virtues of nature."

Europeans often looked upon Americans as noble rustics, almost as wild and free as the so-called savages that inhabited the land before them. Blanchard clearly meant the stereotype as a compliment. His countrymen back in the royal courts of Paris had been so enamored of this vision of Americans that Benjamin Franklin endeared himself by eschewing the typical wigs and frills in favor of a woodsman's fur cap and a modest homespun suit. In playing to such expectations, he managed to secure French aide for the revolution back home.

Commercial spectacle and cross-Atlantic fraternity, however, were not the only goals. Each such aerial feat offered an opportunity, regardless of how briefly, to probe and take measure of the upper atmosphere in a direct way not otherwise possible. Blanchard might well commiserate with modern astronauts who are torn between having to conduct experiments and wanting to simply enjoy the rare view. He performed four specific experiments for others, including measuring his own pulse for Dr. Benjamin Rush and making multiple temperature and barometric observations.

The French reputation for food and the essential wine, even under trying circumstances, was born out by Blanchard. "I strengthened my stomach with a morsel of biscuit and a glass of wine," he wrote, adding, "My trusty companion, the little black dog, partook equally of my care."

Deptford

By using a hydrogen-filled balloon, Blanchard was, as he put it, "fully master of all my ways." While he was still at the mercy of the wind, he could control his descent by carefully releasing the gas via a valve. But first he had to find a suitable spot to land. Out came his spyglass, and he perused the horizon. He had been carried across the Delaware River into southern New Jersey, though he couldn't be exactly certain where. At first, he spied a forest, but seeing no clearings, he continued along until he believed he had found one, only to see it was full of stumps and trees "whose stems were yet too strong not to embarrass and injure my apparel." Throwing off ballast, he rose again and floated farther until he at last found a clearing large enough and set down nearly an hour after lifting off from Philadelphia.

The landing was hard, but all his instruments except a barometer survived unscathed. Happy to be once more on firm ground, the little black dog ran to lap up some water from a puddle but came back to his human companion. Blanchard estimated he still had five or six pounds of biscuits, along with two and a half bottles of wine. He really had no idea where exactly he had landed. All he could see were thick woods all around. So having provisions was more than just French culinary bravado. It was a matter of survival— though not necessarily in the most obvious way.

Blanchard described what happened next:

> With the compass in my hand I formed already plans how to effect my return, after I should have secured my apparatus against accidents, when I heard a noise which informed me of the presence of some person near me. It was indeed a countryman, an inhabitant of this neighbourhood, [sic] who having seen an extraordinary phenomenon in the air had advanced towards the spot, where he supposed it had descended. I spied him and enjoyed his whole surprize [sic], when he saw through a tuft of trees such a monstrous machine, balancing itself, and sinking in proportion as the spirit wherewith it was animated left it. He seemed to be frightened, and I was afraid he would go away again. I let him hear my voice, inviting him to draw near, but either he did not understand me or was retained by a certain distrust;

and at that time I could not quit my balloon. I did better; recollecting that the exhilarating juice of the grape was always amongst mankind the happiest sign of friendship and conciliation, I shewed [sic] him a bottle of wine. So much eagerness on my part inspired him with confidence; he approached, I invited him to drink, he would not venture, I then drank, first, and he followed my example. Becoming soon familiar he assisted me in my operations; when another countryman armed with a gun came to the spot. Never did I see the expression of astonishment so striking as in the features of this man: he dropped his gun and lifted up his hands towards heaven: how I wished to be able to understand him!

The first man explained things to the second—including how he had shared his "excellent wine" and even had a letter from George Washington. Soon, more townspeople arrived, men and women alike. They listened as Washington's letter was read aloud and were soon assisting Blanchard in carefully folding his balloon and carrying it in the basket to a nearby house that had been obscured all along by the trees. He was offered potatoes and a horse that proved too "spirited" for him to ride. So, with a retinue of the curious, he walked to a second house, where he found a horse of a more suitable temperament, and they all proceeded some three miles to a tavern for dinner.

There, he met with Jonathan Penrose, Esquire, who arranged for carriages and a ferry across the Delaware back to where he had started in Philadelphia. He returned with a certificate from those where he landed, reading:

These may certify that we the subscribers saw the bearer, Mr. Blanchard, settle in his balloon in Deptford township, county of Gloucester, in the state of New Jersey, about fifteen miles from Philadelphia, about 10 o'clock 56 minutes, A.M. Witness our hands the ninth day of January, Anno Domini 1793.

> *Everard Bolton,*
> *Joseph Griffith,*
> *Joseph Cheesman,*
> *Samuel Taggart,*
> *Amos Castell,*
> *Zara North*

That the certificate identifies the landing as taking place in Deptford Township is telling. Ever since the first settlement in 1695, it had been called

Bethlehem. Evidently, by the time Blanchard dropped in on them, they were self-identifying as Deptford, even though the state legislature wouldn't officially approve their incorporation as a township under that name until five years later, on February 21, 1798.

The first two names signed on as witnessed, Everard Bolton and Joseph Griffith, would also be signatories to a 1796 petition from Glouster County encouraging the State Assembly to pass an act for the gradual emancipation of slavery—something it would finally do in 1804. Additionally, Griffith's name appears on various petitions looking to use taxes to fund road maintenance and build new bridges.

Blanchard returned to Philadelphia—along with the little black dog, which went back safely to his home. The certificate, along with the two flags, was presented to President Washington, with his sincere thanks for the passport letter that spoke for him to the people of Deptford. He would remain in the United States until 1797.

Fatalities

On his return to France, Blanchard met Marie Madeleine-Sophie Armant, and in 1804, the fifty-one-year-old Jean-Pierre Blanchard married the twenty-six-year-old. They shared a fascination for ballooning, and Sophie Blanchard—as she would become better known—was the first professional female aeronaut. Their marriage, however, lasted only four years. Jean-Pierre suffered a heart attack on February 20, 1808, while in a balloon over The Hague. He died a little more than a year later, on March 7, 1809, from the injuries he sustained having fallen from the basket.

His widow continued ballooning, making more than sixty flights, including for the amusement of Napoleon Bonaparte and King Louis XVIII. If her husband's death wasn't enough to make the point that this was all still a perilous business, she lost consciousness herself and risked freezing from the high altitudes she achieved. Once, when her balloon crash-landed in a swamp, she was almost drowned. In 1819, however, her luck also ran out. During an exhibition at Tivoli Gardens in Paris, the fireworks she launched from the basket ignited the hydrogen gas in her balloon. The burning craft crashed into a roof, and she died from the fall—becoming the first female aviation fatality.

Back in the United States, Deptford retained its rural appeal in the centuries since its then-thick forests bedeviled Blanchard's first two landing

THIS PLAQUE REDEDICATES THE LANDING
SITE OF JEAN PIERRE BLANCHARD'S
ASCENSION FROM PHILADELPHIA, ON THIS
THE 200TH ANNIVERSARY OF

"THE FIRST AIR VOYAGE IN AMERICA"

PRESENTED ON JANUARY 9, 1993

BY

FAVIA 200 INC. & THE
TOWNSHIP OF DEPTFORD, NJ

Opposite: Sophie Blanchard was the first female aeronaut. *U.S. Library of Congress.*

Above: This plaque was erected in 1993 on the 100th anniversary of Blanchard's flight. *Courtesy of the author.*

Left: The Blanchard plaque sits near the Clement Oak, named after the family who used to own the property. The white oak tree was mentioned in land records as early as 1678. The plaque about it has since been moved. *Courtesy of the author.*

99

Today, the Blanchard plaque and Clement Oak are crowded by the back of a Walmart Supercenter. *Courtesy of the author.*

attempts. Parts of it have been whittled away to form neighboring towns, reducing the original 106 square miles to under 18 today. These days, it's better known for being home to the state's largest shopping mall or as the hometown of rock musician and songwriter Patti Smith. But the community still takes a sense of civic pride from its unexpected role in America's first manned flight—and the hospitality it showed the Frenchman so curiously dropped amongst them. Township signs, stationery and a water tower sport a trademarked hot-air balloon logo.

Despite this, modernity has come to cramp the landing spot, where bronze plaques explain its significance. It now sits behind a Walmart Supercenter. There is one survivor, however, to remind people of the significance of that patch of dirt—the Clement Oak is old enough to have been witness to the strange contraption sailing down into the clearing.

Jean-Pierre Blanchard, with his effusive fondness for America and Americans, would likely be pleased to know that the descendants of the countrymen who welcomed him still remember.

Chapter 6

MOSES IN CAPE MAY

"There's two things I got a right to, and these are Death and Liberty," Harriet Tubman was said to have declared. "One or the other I mean to have."

Few people have come to embody the cause of abolitionism, heart and soul, both then and now, like Harriet Tubman. And few have been as unlikely. Yet what most people don't know, and historians gloss over, is an interesting tie she has with South Jersey.

Like the stories of most people who emerge from obscurity to do great things, the circumstances of her life have been mythologized as she became as much a symbol as a historical figure. The irony is that what facts we can be sure of hardly need such romantic polishing.

She was born Araminta "Minty" Ross, though *when* is a question. Slave births were rarely recorded, leaving historians and biographers to use circumstantial evidence. Biographer Kate Larson came up with 1822 based on a midwife payment, a runaway slave advertisement and other documents. Jean Humez wrote that "the best current evidence suggests that Tubman was born in 1820, but it might have been a year or two later." That Tubman herself didn't know seems evident from Civil War pension records where she gave her year of birth variously as 1820, 1822 and 1825. Her death certificate claimed she was born in 1815, while her gravestone puts it at 1820.

Regardless of when she was born, however, one thing was certain: by the laws of her native Dorchester County, Maryland, she was born a slave. Her mother, Harriet Green—known as Rit—was enslaved, working as a cook in the home of Edward and Mary Pattison Brodess. Her father, Ben, was a woodsman on a nearby plantation owned by Dr. Anthony Thompson. Evidence shows that her maternal grandmother, Modesty, was abducted from Africa, and the young Araminta was told her ancestors were of the Ashanti people, in what is today Ghana.

Court records indicate Rit and Ben were married in 1808, and together they would have nine children. The concept of "family," however, was something of a fragile commodity for slaves. Edward Brodess would sell off three of Rit and Ben's daughters, never to be seen again. When Brodess came up with a buyer from Georgia to buy Rit's youngest son, Moses, however,

Harriet Tubman. *Circa 1885, H. Seymour Squyer, National Portrait Gallery.*

something inside her at last snapped. With the aide of fellow slaves and freed blacks, the boy was hid for about a month before Brodess and the Georgia buyer came to the slave quarters to take him. Rit was said to have declared that "the first man that comes into my house, I will split his head open!" Evidently, there was enough in her tone or her look that told the men she wasn't bluffing. The buyer probably thought it was more trouble than it was worth and abandoned the deal. But Araminta was watching, and most of her eventual biographers agree that witnessing this act of overt—and successful—defiance by her mother inspired her lifelong proactive resistance.

A reminder of just how brutal life could be for a slave was only as distant as the scars on her flesh from the five lashes she had once received as a girl. Such abuse started early. Somewhere around only five or six years old, she was hired out as a nursemaid to watch over the sleeping baby of a "Miss Susan." If the child awoke and started crying, Araminta was whipped.

The devotion to resistance that emerged from such experiences was deeply rooted. She would run away—for at least five days on one occasion. But that spirit of defiance would also be refined by a resourcefulness that would prove effective. Even as a girl, she figured out she could deflect the pain of beatings with the padding of extra layers of clothing.

Araminta's adolescence was punctuated by acts of marked callousness by owners to whom she had been hired out by Brodess. One, a planter named James Cook, sent her out to check his muskrat traps, even though she was sick, as it turned out, with the measles. When she became too sick to work, Cook sent her back to Brodess. Fortunately, Rit was apparently able to be home long enough to nurse her back to health. That wasn't a given for slave families. Her father worked on another plantation altogether, and Rit's responsibilities kept her in "the big house," tending to the Brodess family's needs instead of her own. An extended family of relatives or unrelated fellow slaves might pitch in, and the older children were expected to take care of the younger. But being sent off when hired out strained the already tenuous family ties, and Araminta would long remember the pangs of homesickness that were part of her youth.

Perhaps the greatest physical insult to her person, while not strictly intentional, was the one that would make her both an unlikely and yet driven hero. One day, a teenage Araminta was sent off for supplies at the dry goods store by one of the many men to whom she was hired out. The otherwise routine chore was enlivened when an irate white man stormed in. One of the black men also in the shop, he claimed, had left the fields without permission—and he meant to take him back, by force if needed. When the black man resisted, the furious overseer demanded that Araminta help restrain him. But she refused, and the slave managed to slip away. As he ran, the overseer grabbed a two-pound weight from the shop scale and hurled it at him. Unfortunately for Araminta, his aim was off, and it struck her in the head instead.

If the overseer felt bad, it was likely only because he had damaged another man's property. She was returned, bleeding and unconscious. For two days, she lay on a bench without medical attention. The man who hired her tried to send her back out into the fields, despite the blood still trickling down into her eyes. Unable to work, she was a liability to the man who hired her from Brodess, and he sent her back. Edward Brodess also saw her as a liability and tried selling her. He found no buyers for what they probably would have seen as damaged goods.

She would survive, of course—later, she would quip that it was her mass of unruly, uncombed hair that probably kept it from killing her outright. But she would never be the same. The blow left her with seizures where she would seem to fall into a deep sleep, though she claimed to be aware of her surroundings. It is speculated that she suffered what's known as temporal lobe epilepsy. It must have scared her family to no end when it first started happening.

The timing of the injury, it would turn out, was significant. She had always been a religious child. On those occasions when they could be together at home, her mother read to her out of the Bible. Tales of deliverance from the Old Testament likely resonated with her. By the time she was a teenager, Araminta was drawn deeper into religion. So when after her injury she started having what she described as visions or vivid dreams, she concluded they had to have been divinely inspired. Brain damage–inspired revelations aside, however, Araminta was no fool.

Anthony Thomas, who owned her father, had stipulated that Ben would be freed at age forty-five. He was manumitted in 1840, though in reality, he was probably closer to fifty-five. But this got Araminta thinking—perhaps there was a similar stipulation that came when the Brodess family bought Rit? There was only one way to find out, so she managed to scrape together the five-dollar fee for a white lawyer to research her mother's status. Just as she had suspected, he found that there was a similar stipulation for Rit in the will of a former owner. Additionally, if she was free, her children were, too. Though bound to honor it, the Brodess family had ignored the clause. It must have deeply frustrated Araminta to know that she didn't have the resources to seek redress.

So life went on as before. Knowing no other existence than the one in front of him, Ben continued to work for the Thompson family with the somewhat elevated title of "foreman" and as a timber estimator. And Rit remained in bondage in the Brodess household.

Harriet

Next to nothing is known about John Tubman, other than that he was a free black man who married Araminta in 1844. Such "blended marriages" between enslaved and free blacks were not uncommon, though it may have been an added complication in their relationship. Status came down through one's mother, meaning any offspring would be considered slaves. Some biographers have speculated that they may have planned to buy Araminta's freedom after marriage.

When exactly Araminta made the determination to be henceforth known as "Harriet" is uncertain, though some believe it may have been around the time of her marriage, suggesting it was indeed part of a larger plan of buying her freedom—a new name for a new life. Others think it came later, when she decided on her own to escape. Others, still, wondered if it wasn't part of a religious conversion or some traditional honoring of her mother or a deceased relative.

In everyday terms, it really didn't matter much. To the Brodess family, she was still Minty. And by 1849, she was also back in poor enough health to again be considered a liability. Edward Brodess tried unsuccessfully once more to sell her. The threat of being removed from her family was made all the more galling to her because she knew how her master had cheated them all out of their freedom. Having nowhere to turn, she sought help from her God—with a startling result. "I prayed all night long for my master," she remembered, "till the first of March; and all the time he was bringing people to look at me, and trying to sell me." At first, her prayers seemed to fall on deaf ears, until one buyer looked rather serious. With even greater desperation, she decided to tweak her request. "First of March I began to pray, 'Oh Lord, if you ain't never going to change that man's heart, kill him, Lord, and take him out of the way.'"

Despite all the mistreatment, she still felt a twinge of regret when a week later Edward Brodess actually did die. Be careful what you wish for, the old saying went, and it was definitely true for Harriet. With Brodress's death, it was then almost a certainty that the family would be split up and sold off with the rest of his property. There was nothing now to hold her back.

Death or freedom, as she said, was all she had left.

The Underground Railroad

Harriet Tubman's decision to master her own fate was fraught with risk. As awful as the prospects of staying were, running away could get a slave killed. Additionally, as an example to others contemplating the same thing, it was not uncommon for various forms of torture to be inflicted before execution. John Tubman tried to dissuade her, though it was easy for him to say as a free man.

In September 1849, she had been hired out to the same Anthony Thompson who owned her father. In all likelihood, two of her brothers, Ben

(Jr.) and Henry were also working there. On the seventeenth, they slipped away with the intention of heading to the free states they had heard were up north. It would, however, be an abortive effort. It could be that Ben, who may have just become a father, was the first to have second thoughts. But both brothers determined to return, and despite her protests, they got their sister to come back with them. They had been gone at least two weeks, as the widowed Eliza Brodess advertised them as runaways after that time, offering rewards of $100 for each. It isn't clear if they were punished when they got back, though the fact that they returned on their own may have mitigated any thoughts of a death penalty.

Whatever the case, it seems clear that coming back was never Harriet's idea. A few days later, she left again, this time without her brothers. But before she departed, she wanted to get word to Rit of her plans. She made use of an ingenious system of communication that slaves had employed for generations—singing. Rhythmic work songs helped set the pace and made repetitive labor less odious. Spirituals invoked the rewards of heaven, drawing on the obviously attractive Old Testament themes of deliverance. But it also meant that, if individuals or groups could sing loud enough to be heard on the next farm, coded information could be passed along. To the overseers, it just looked like happy Negroes who sure did love to sing. They didn't understand that when Harriet's friend, a fellow slave named Mary, was singing, "I'm bound for the promised land," it carried a more literal meaning.

There is a romantic version of her journey that has become part of the popular mythology. Granted, it does have an appeal—a strong black woman all on her own, seizing her own freedom, guided only by the North Star, her visions and her wits. The historic reality, however, seems to have been more practical than mystical. The interjection of a white woman living nearby who helped get her on her way is at first jarring to the sense of the heroic. And yet, it is far more indicative of who Tubman was as a person. For one thing, it shows that any bitterness over her treatment at white hands hadn't kept her from trusting someone based on race. This perspective would enable her in years to come to cultivate important alliances with some of the country's most powerful white men in service to the cause.

At the same time, she also entered the murky world of the Underground Railroad. This was a truly remarkable secret society of proactive abolitionists, freed slaves and even slaves still in bondage who bled the slave states a handful of slaves at a time, with a network of safe houses to help them escape. It was both informal and well organized, drawing on the terminology of the most high-tech industry of the day, the railroads, mixed with religious metaphors. Escaping slaves were "passengers" or "cargo," guided by "conductors," on the "Gospel Train," heading to the "promised land."

A combination of geography and demographics would ensure that South Jersey would play a significant role in the operation. Straddling between the urban centers of Philadelphia and New York, and its proximity to the slave state of Delaware, made it a logical pathway for fugitive slaves—all the more so given the strong influence of Quakers, who had long embraced abolitionism. When the Maryland slave Levin Still was able to purchase his freedom, he came to Burlington County to settle, joined by his wife, Charity, and their four children when she escaped. A son, William, born there in 1821, would go on to work with the Philadelphia Anti-Slavery Society and become the "Father of the Underground Railroad," conducting as many as sixty slaves a month into the North as he cultivated his network.

While many would continue on up into Canada (particularly after the Fugitive Slave Act's passage made recapture a real threat), many former slaves found South Jersey to their liking. There was land to farm, and the geography was suitable for someone who didn't want to be found. Some twenty-three black settlements dotted New Jersey, with most around the Delaware Valley, which became known as the "Cradle of Emancipation."

Tubman's exact route isn't known. It wasn't until well after the fact that she would even talk about it, lest she yet jeopardize the safety of others who might still use it. Secrecy was paramount, and even conductors didn't know the full extent of the network so as to contain the damage to the whole should any single line be infiltrated or compromised. But she probably worked her way north along the Choptank River through Delaware and on up into Pennsylvania, to Philadelphia—a journey of about ninety miles on foot, taking as many as three weeks.

"When I found I had crossed that line," she later recalled of entering Pennsylvania, "I looked at my hands to see if I was the same person. There was such a glory over everything; the sun came like gold through the trees, and over the fields, and I felt like I was in Heaven."

Settling in Philadelphia, she might have been pleasantly surprised at the world beyond the bubble of the plantation. There was an established radical sentiment within the antislavery community, started by William Lloyd Garrison, calling for an *immediate* end to slavery—no more of the piecemeal approach of gradual emancipation. Slavery was being actively derided as a moral outrage from theist and secularists alike; women's groups called not only for the end of slavery but also redress of oppressions

Top: William Lloyd Garrison. *U.S. National Archives.*

Bottom: William Still. The Underground Railroad from Slavery to Freedom, *by Wilbur Henry Siebert, Albert Bushnell Hart, 2nd edition, published by Macmillan, 1898.*

inflicted specifically on their gender. It must have been a hopeful revelation to resourceful Harriet Tubman.

At the Anti-Slavery Society headquartered in Philadelphia, she probably first met William Still. As a clerk, he was responsible for interviewing fugitives who had come through the network. Later, she was known to have stayed with Still's family when traveling through the city. She also formed a friendship with James and Lucretia Mott, influential Quaker abolitionist and women's rights advocates. Likely, either Still or one of the Motts—probably without much resistance—recruited her to work with them on the Underground Railroad.

Harriet Tubman's joy at reaching the "promised land" was bittersweet. With something perhaps akin to a survivor's guilt, she remembered her family still in bondage. It was enough to make her entertain a very dangerous idea—she would go *back*, risking capture and probably death, to use her practical experience with the Underground Railroad to help them, too, escape.

In December 1850, such plans were pushed into action. Her extended family included freed blacks, who were able to get word to her of the impending sale of her niece, Kassiah, with her six-year-old son, James Alfred, and an infant, also named Araminta, thrown into the bargain. Tubman would have to act fast. Kassiah's husband, a free black man named John Bowley, attended the auction and made the winning bid. If any of the white men eyed him with suspicion, they were correct. He really didn't have the money—he was buying time so Kassiah and the children could escape to a nearby Underground Railroad safe house. Under cover of night, they took a log canoe some sixty miles to Baltimore, where Harriet Tubman was waiting to conduct them to Philadelphia.

Emboldened by her success, she went back again that spring of 1851, this time for her brother, Moses, and two other unnamed men. She had made important contacts, such as Quaker abolitionist Thomas Garrett, who was always getting into trouble even as an old man with the authorities in his hometown of Wilmington, Delaware, for assisting fugitive slaves. Success bred confidence, and each trip led to plans for one more. She extended her services beyond her own family, to anyone seeking freedom.

Such trips were dangerous, but they were also costly. A large group of black people traveling on their own would raise suspicions, so some of the process included walking at night or along secluded streambeds or paths that headed in the right direction. But when she traveled alone or just had one or two people with her, it was possible to speed things up by traveling by carriage or boat. Trusted slaves were often sent off on their own to town on their master's errands. So a black woman traveling alone wasn't automatically a red flag, allowing her to risk hiring transport from unsuspecting conveyances. Keeping with the railroad theme, the network had "stockholders"—people who donated money and supplies. But finding funding was a constant worry.

Tubman was able to find enough work in Philadelphia to maintain an apartment and buy necessities. She was also responsible for the room and board of her young fugitive nephew, James Bowley, then living and going to school in Philadelphia. Beyond this, however, she needed money for her rescue work. In the early 1850s, she evidently became aware of opportunities on the other side of the Delaware River in South Jersey.

Moses in Cape May

It isn't an intended slight that South Jersey's connection with Tubman gets short shrift in biographies. In a life as broad in scope as hers, it is something of a minor detail. And yet, it played an important role for her at the time.

Vacationers from Philadelphia had been heading to the southernmost tip of New Jersey since the mid-eighteenth century, making it the oldest seaside resort in America. The resulting tourist economy was robust but also seasonal. Then as now, for a couple months each summer, the hotels and restaurants bustle with business. They hired temporary staffs, all eager to make as much money as possible before the winter downtime. Each summer, from as early as 1849 until as late as 1853, among them was Harriet Tubman.

That she worked there has been repeated many times by her biographers, usually afforded a line or two at most. Among the first was a New York children's book writer, Sarah Hopkins Bradford. In 1869, she published her first adult book, *Scenes in the Life of Harriet Tubman*, drawing from interviews with Tubman herself. "She came to Philadelphia, and worked in hotels, in clubs, and afterwards at Cape May," Bradford wrote. She later mentions that Tubman worked as a cook for private families, though it isn't clear if she meant in Cape May specifically. The book sold well enough that Bradford returned to the subject in 1886 with *Harriet Tubman, Moses of Her People*. The same general statement was repeated, adding no more details. And so it has been repeated ever since.

Given the clandestine nature of her mission, finding evidence of her time there is like chasing a ghost. Nevertheless, it is possible to indulge in some reasonable speculation. Given the rather limited career options open to a black woman in the beginning years of the 1850s, it seems safe to presume she would have found employment as a cook, maid or washerwoman. It would also make sense for her to adopt a false name, further obscuring her presence even if any contemporary records were still extant. In all likelihood, she would have desired to simply blend into the background of dark-faced domestics, hidden away behind the scenes, collecting her pay, making her plans. As a fugitive slave, bringing any sort of attention to herself could be risky. So, if she had been working at the Atlantic House hotel on July 31, 1850, it is to be wondered what she would have made of something that happened in the ballroom that evening.

A white Marylander reportedly attempted to take a glass of wine from a tray for a female companion when a black waiter "rudely repulsed him." When the man berated the waiter, he responded by daring the "damned Southerner" to try to come take the glass, making like he was about to strike him. Someone intervened, however, and both men withdrew for the moment. When the ball was over, however, the insulted white man punched the waiter, and a brawl between black servants and the party of white Baltimoreans ensued. The southerners prevailed, forcing the other side to retreat, but they re-formed out in front, brandishing knives and clubs, daring them to come out and try their luck again. The southerners remained indoors, and the mob dispersed. Rumors arrived with breakfast the next morning of a meeting having been held by the Negroes, resolving to seek revenge on all southerners and the Baltimoreans in particular. The ladies of the party convinced their male counterparts to leave Cape May that night to avoid more trouble.

The event made the *Baltimore Patriot* newspaper, back in slaveholding Maryland, where members of Tubman's family remained in bondage. Curiously, the whole thing was played down by the *Easton Star*, out of Easton, Maryland. It characterized the event as a "slight difficulty," where the waiters "talked somewhat of retaliation," and after the waiters involved were fired, "[t]he visitors on the island gave no consequence to the affair whatsoever."

The first account sounds like it came from the aggrieved Baltimoreans themselves and the latter from a hotel owner worried about losing business! But if Tubman was witness or heard about it at all, perhaps she took a little guilty pleasure in hearing how the Marylanders were driven away.

The point, of course, is that we just don't know. We don't know where specifically she worked. We don't know if she confided in any fellow black servants about the adventuresome and risky life she led when she wasn't cooking or washing sheets. Indeed, we wouldn't know she had been in Cape May at all had it not been for her mentioning it in passing.

It is, of course, arguable how strong or important this New Jersey connection really is. Certainly, it has been snatched up and repeated in lists of South Jersey and Cape May history trivia—a curious factoid of questionable relevance. Yet there is a practical importance to her time here, however brief, however obscured. The money handed over to her by presumably unknowing bosses or slipped into her hand as a tip had made a rather critical difference in real people's lives. Examining how she spent it is important to understanding that context.

"It was in this pleasure cove that Tubman cooked for families and hotel kitchens to build up her war chest," described biographer Catherine Clinton in her 2004 *Harriet Tubman: The Road to Freedom.* "During the summer of 1850," George Sullivan wrote in his 2001 *Harriet Tubman*, "Harriet worked in a hotel in Cape May, New Jersey. She carefully saved the money she earned. She needed it to buy food and supplies for another trip into the South. This time her goal was to bring her husband back north with her."

Harriet Tubman told Sarah Hopkins Bradford only marginally more about her husband than she had about her time in Cape May. John Tubman doesn't appear to have taken her ambition to escape very seriously. Bradford related that he likened her scheme to a folk story about a man called Cudjo, who would only laugh at a joke after everyone else was done—meaning Harriet spoke bravely, but he didn't believe she would take the risk in the face of real danger. It is also possible that he saw no reasons, as a free man, that he should uproot himself from the life he had known, abandoning friends and family. Besides, perhaps someday he could earn enough money to solve the problem by buying her freedom.

But with Edward Brodess's death and seeing others dragged off, Harriett didn't feel like she could wait around. It was then that she made that first abortive attempt at escape with her brothers and then finally left all on her own. Despite John Tubman calling her a fool, the fact that she really loved him was demonstrated by her willingness to come back for him. Her first two rescues took her only as far as Baltimore and Cambridge, Maryland—to go anywhere near Dorchester County, where someone might recognize her, was far too risky. Yet that's what she needed to do in order to find John that fall of 1851.

There are two versions of what happened next, or at least how it happened. Both agree that she disguised herself as a man. George Sullivan's account, however, is a bit more melodramatic. In his description, she knocked on

John's door, and it took a moment for him to realize it was his wife in men's clothing. Shocked, he invited her in, and then she noticed the woman sitting by the fire. He introduced her as Caroline—his new wife. Charles L. Blockson, in his 1987 book, *The Underground Railroad: First-Person Narratives of Escapes to Freedom in the North*, sets a less dramatic scene. Tubman was hiding out and had heard from others that he had remarried. She sent word anyway that she was there to take him north, but he refused to join her. There was no face-to-face confrontation.

Whether she appeared on his doorstep or not, John Tubman wasn't necessarily the unfaithful villain hinted at by some biographies. He may have considered his wife's plans foolhardy and saw her as having abandoned him. When she returned, two years had passed, and as he had no reason to think he would ever see her again, his remarriage wasn't impossible to understand. Still, it must have been a palpably bitter disappointment for her—particularly given the dangers she risked to come back.

If John didn't want to leave, there were others who did, and she left with several fugitive slaves, whom she deposited in Philadelphia. There were other relatives still in bondage she wanted to go back for, but out of the painful experience of that last trip emerged a realization: there were many metaphorical brothers and sisters in need of someone to lead them to the promised land. She threw herself into her work as a conductor on the Underground Railroad. In December 1851, she went back for eleven more, and there is evidence to suggest that among the safe houses they used on the way to Canada was one owned by Frederick Douglass—the beginnings of a lifelong friendship and fruitful partnership in the cause.

Over the next eleven years, she made thirteen trips back into slave territory, ultimately guiding about three hundred slaves to freedom. She had a remarkable ability to think on her feet. Using a tightly drawn bonnet to hide her face and carrying two chickens, she looked like just another Negro on an errand. When, however, she saw a former owner coming the other way, she yanked on the string that held the birds' legs, creating a diversion to draw the man's eyes away from her own. In another instance, a different former master was on the same train, so she snatched a newspaper and pretended to be reading it—she was illiterate, but the ex-master was none the wiser. She understood this was no game but a life or death proposition. She carried a pistol, not only for protection but also as "incentive" for anyone in a group having second thoughts about escaping. When the crying of a teething baby threatened to give them away, she produced a bottle of morphine to soothe the infant. It might seem counterintuitive to run expeditions in the cold of winter, but the nights were long and people tended to remain indoors, lessening the chance of being spotted. She even learned to time escapes such that a few days would pass before the runaway slave ads would appear in the newspapers, buying them extra time to get that much more distance between them.

It is to be wondered what those ornery Baltimoreans vacationing in Cape May would have thought had they known this woman was amongst them— that perhaps *their* money was going toward her missions. To many, she would be eyed as an uppity enemy, breaking the law in some misguided ideal that Negroes were meant by God to be anything but property.

To those she led, however, she began to become known by a fitting codename: "Moses." And Moses had paid their way with money she earned in Cape May.

"I Go to Prepare a Place for You"

In one of those seemingly anachronistic overlaps that come up in history, a woman who would come to symbolize the Civil Rights struggle for the twentieth century was born a month before Harriet Tubman, a symbol from the nineteenth century, would die. Rosa Parks was born on February 4, 1913, in Tuskegee, Alabama, and Tubman passed away in Auburn, New York, on March 14, 1913.

Between the early 1850s and 1913, the arc of Tubman's career took her ever deeper into active—even radical—resistance to slavery. In 1858, for example, she encountered the white abolitionist John Brown. Claiming similar divine inspirations as Tubman, he saw himself as the spark that would ignite a general slave revolt throughout the South. Toward that end, he devised a plan to raid the arsenal at Harper's Ferry, Virginia, seizing the weapons that would be needed and providing the inspiration for like-minded others. Tubman was a font of practical intelligence and offered to help recruit the manpower. The authorities, however, became tipped off, and the raid was a failure, ending in the killing or capture of all involved. Those arrested, including Brown himself, were tried and convicted of treason and hanged. Tubman did not participate in the actual raid. While her whereabouts are unclear, speculation ranges from her having been ill to being up in Canada recruiting men for the cause.

Whatever the case, she would have opportunity enough to prove her mettle with the outbreak of the Civil War. She understood this was *the* best opportunity to crush slavery once and for all, becoming frustrated with

Lincoln's early resistance to emancipation. Not only did she head into the South to assist newly freed or escaped slaves, but she would also play an active role in the support of the Union troops. She was a frequent feature at the camps around the Port Royal, South Carolina area, working as a nurse. But her greatest asset was her working knowledge of the terrain and identifying pockets of support. She provided intelligence to the army brass, including Colonel James Montgomery on his capture of Jacksonville, Florida, and Colonel Robert Gould Shaw, who raised the first all-Negro regiment.

On the morning of June 2, 1863, she guided three Union steamboats around Confederate mines in South Carolina's Combahee River. Plantations throughout the area were burned by Union troops as the shrill whistle of the steamboat was the signal for some seven hundred slaves to board and be taken north. "I never saw such a sight," she remembered later. The Combahee River Raid brought her national attention. Newspapers celebrated her "patriotism, sagacity, energy, [and] ability."

She allegedly served Colonel Robert Gould Shaw his last meal before the fatal 1868 assault on Fort Wagner and helped collect the corpses when the battle was done.

Harriet Tubman spent the war—and even a few months afterward—volunteering her services to the Union army, as well as assisting fugitive slaves. "Volunteering" is the operative word there. She never took a salary, and it wouldn't be until 1899 that the government even acknowledged its debt to her service and approved her request for a pension. Like the black soldiers she recruited out of the ranks of her fugitive slaves, she was up against the prejudices of the day when it came to being equally compensated for their risks and sacrifices.

In a twist of fate, on the way back home after the war, she would suffer a similar indignity as Rosa Parks. She was on her way to a house in Auburn, New York, that she had purchased in 1859 from then senator William H. Seward, who went on to be Lincoln's secretary of state. A conductor on the train she was riding insisted that she move from her seat to the smoking car. She refused, explaining that after her service to the country, she had earned the right to sit there. He cursed her and attempted to pull her out of the seat; other passengers helped him finally throw her back into the car, breaking her arm in the process.

Then, in 1873, she was taken in by swindlers who claimed they had a cache of gold smuggled out of South Carolina—many southerners buried their gold during the war, and black men were pressed into digging graves, so it was not implausible. But the gold didn't exist, and the two men knocked her

Harriet Tubman late in life, circa 1911. *U.S. Library of Congress.*

out with chloroform and stole the money she had borrowed to pay them. It was an insult added to injury. Her charity had left her nearly penniless. One positive thing to come out of her state was meeting Nelson Davis, a black Civil War veteran and bricklayer, whom she took in as a boarder to help pay the bills in Auburn. A relationship developed, and they were married on March 18, 1869, later adopting a baby girl named Gertie.

In the later years of her life, she became involved with the African Methodist Episcopal Zion Church, donating part of the land to be used as a home for aged and indigent blacks, which she herself became, and was admitted in 1911. The sleeping spells she had suffered from the head injury grew worse—so bad, in fact, that she agreed to brain surgery in Boston, which alleviated it somewhat.

Her frail and aged form was at last conquered by pneumonia on March 10, 1913. It was said that her last words were: "I go to prepare a place for you." She left behind a truly remarkable legacy—as well as one last Cape May mystery.

Settlement?

It isn't clear who wrote it, but there is a lengthy obituary that began to make the rounds of the newspapers following Harriet Tubman's death. It struck all the themes one might imagine such a summary might—how she had led hundreds of her fellow Negroes from bondage at great personal risk ("the Moses of her people"); how she had earned the esteem and hearty friendship of such nineteenth-century luminaries as Ralph Waldo Emerson, William Lloyd Garrison, Bishop Phillips Brooks, reformer politician Horace Mann, Frederick Douglas, reformer Gerrit Smith and even the martyred John Brown (all of whom she had outlived); it cited a specific example of her peril and spirit in Troy, New York, where she and a gathered mob bodily intervened in the return of a fugitive slave named Charles Nalle and skillfully fought off attacks to her person. Perhaps the simplest testimony to her effectiveness was embodied in the $40,000 reward offered by southern plantation owners for her capture, with the added dramatic but earnest "dead or alive." And yet she returned again and again to the territories where that bounty had been put up.

But tucked between all that and a summary of her service to the Union during the Civil War are two curious lines:

> *As the slave-owners had paid agents in Philadelphia, she decided to establish her free slaves elsewhere, and started a settlement at Cape May, N.J., in 1852. This place was successfully managed by her with the aid of Thomas Garrett, the Quaker abolitionist, of Wilmington, Del.*

What makes this so curious is that word "settlement." None of the biographies of Tubman—including those based on interviews with her—mention anything that might qualify as a settlement in Cape May. Certainly, there were numerous enclaves where fugitive slaves on the Underground Railroad would find safety in numbers—"parallel communities," as Dennis Rizzo described them in his study of such places. Yet none has any known associations with Tubman when it came to its founding.

She certainly knew the Thomas Garrett mentioned. Indeed, they were of the same hardcore spirit. He was estranged from his orthodox Pennsylvania Quaker family, having taken their embrace of abolitionism but not their pacifism. He respected William Lloyd Garrison but could not agree with his turn-the-other-cheek nonviolent approach. Like Tubman, when someone attacked Garrett physically, he had no qualms about cracking heads.

Indeed, he held somewhat prophetically that slavery would only be abolished through civil war. He had moved to Delaware where he made his living from the iron and hardware trade and managed to openly carry on as a safe house without getting in trouble until 1848, when he and a fellow Quaker were arrested and heavily fined for helping a fugitive family. He managed to raise the $4,500 and went right on with his activities.

Thomas Garrett.

Tubman passed through his station many times with her charges. Evidently, Ben and Rit were still living in Maryland assisting with her work until 1858, when her father was threatened with arrest for harboring a fugitive family. Garrett financed her trip to retrieve them up to Canada. Yet there does not appear to be evidence that he established a *settlement* in or near Cape May, either with or without her.

Her hometown newspaper, the *Auburn Citizen*, also included an odd mention. "She established a headquarters at Cape May, N.J.," it claimed, "and in the fall of 1852 disappeared from her usual haunts to reappear in a few weeks with nine fugitives."

Words like "settlement" and "headquarters" suggest a more substantial operation than a summer job to finance later trips. "With Thomas Garrett," it continued, "the well-known Quaker abolitionists of Wilmington, Del., she aided in freeing over 3,000 slaves, her personal conduct taking 300 of them into Canada. Through Garrett she met leaders in the Anti-Slavery movement and soon had established her Underground Railway, stations being located in every abolitionist center wherein fugitives were concealed and fed by day and aided on their way to Suspension Bridge and Canada by night."

Alas, while they may be concise and convenient summaries, obituaries often get it wrong. Aside from the potential for inadvertent errors introduced by a reporter on a deadline, consider it was 1913. While there were still some Civil War veterans left to shuffle in Memorial Day parades, the world Tubman knew must have seemed like a different universe by then. Early automobiles were starting to sputter down streets; the Wright brothers' first flight was already a decade old; HMS *Titanic* sank the year before; rudimentary wireless crackled through the air; and the telephone was established technology. The details surrounding her days at Cape May—minor in the full context of her long life—were sixty-one years old. Recording them with any real fidelity after all that time would be a tall task.

Still.

Given the necessarily secretive nature of her work, it is tempting to wonder if there wasn't more to the story of the summers Moses came to Cape May.

Chapter 7
THE LAST TEA PARTY

There is little doubt that the birth of the United States was midwifed by some very smart and brave students of the Enlightenment. We remember and celebrate them to this day, and even when their human failings are revealed, it tends only to render what they achieved all the more remarkable.

Yet this was not the immaculate conception of our creation myths. There were often seamier concurrent narratives characterized by mob violence, strong-arm intimidation, terrorism (arguably) and punitive vandalism (certainly).

These perhaps less-than-noble episodes have been rationalized and polished in our collective memories, even elevated as worthy of pride and (often misguided) emulation. Among those that have become legend is the so-called Boston Tea Party. While rather iconic, it was actually just one of several similar spasms of civil disobedience to fatally strain the ties between the American colonies and Great Britain—and would echo into a South Jersey village.

The Stamp Act

Exactly why the Americans of the latter half of the eighteenth century felt so compelled to break free from Great Britain has been grist for historical debate. At least one spark to the fuse was an inflated view we had developed of ourselves and our role within the British Empire. Such a self-image likely had several causes. Economically, the vast natural resources of the continent guaranteed us a critical place in the lucrative Atlantic "trade triangle" between England, the Caribbean and North America. We also supplied the raw materials for the military adventurism that had grown the empire. Take just one example of how America was still possessed of the sorts of forests that could produce timber tall enough for the masts on the ships with which Britannia ruled the waves—forests that had been largely depleted on the English isle itself. Beyond that was the matter of sheer scale. Claims and competition from Natives and French settlements notwithstanding, there was a *lot* of real estate for the colonists to grow into. It took no great leap of the imagination on either side of the Atlantic to forecast a day when the center of imperial gravity would shift to the colonies as Americans outnumbered Englishmen.

And that was part of it—they were *Americans*, a separate identity with an often abstract and traditional tie to England.

Americans had spent a handful of generations carving thriving enclaves of European-styled civilization from a wilderness. Children were born, grew up and even died there, without having ever known their king or queen beyond a profile on their coins. England was an abstract place for many by the mid-1700s—not quite "home." Nevertheless, they were also taught that their monarch was good and wise and took pride in reigning over free men, regardless of where in the empire they happened to live. They lived with an odd dual identity—at once both American by birth and yet proud to be British by nationality. Still, given the abstraction of the ties to England for many, it is little wonder which one they would choose when circumstances pushed them to take sides.

Nevertheless, those who maintained a British identity—founded on cultural and economic interests—did so with the assumption that they were due, as a matter of birthright, the same rights and considerations as anyone born and living in England proper.

Conservatives in England, however, saw things rather differently. America might be vast, but it was still a *colony* and, like any other colony, existed at the prerogative of, and for the enrichment of, the mother country. There was a balance of power to be maintained, and London was *the* center of the imperial universe. Then, as now, the analogy has often been drawn to the relationship between a parent (England) and a child (America). But it seems more accurate to think of the dynamic as that existing between a master (England) and a servant (America). A master might be benevolent toward his servant, but he could never suffer to consider him as an equal. It was the stratified, class-conscious mindset of the culture, only writ here on the global scale.

In the back of everyone's minds, of course, was the seeming inevitability that America's population would one day outnumber that of England's, giving the provincials more power and influence in Parliament. Up to the mid-1700s, what had largely kept that day at bay had been their traditional rival: France. Where the English colonies tended to cling to the East Coast, French settlements and forts dotted the Hudson Bay and Great Lakes region in the north and the Mississippi Valley to the south. They had hopes of connecting the two in the Ohio Valley, effectively shutting England's back door to the interior of the continent. When England and France went to war in Europe, America became a de facto front and an excuse to fight for superior positioning.

But between 1754 and 1763, war broke out in, and over control of, America itself. The English called it the French and Indian War—the "and Indian" part coming from how both sides fought with respective Native American allies. An English victory in that conflict at last gave them control over all of North America. But with that prize also came two headaches. One was that the French barrier to America becoming more populous and powerful was gone. The second was that the war had come close to bankrupting England.

The former would be dealt with by legislation limiting settlement to east of the Appalachian Mountains, ostensibly in deference to Native fears of encroachment. While the policy made a lot of Americans who were eager to seek new territory angry, it was how the latter issue was handled that would bring things to a violent head.

Funds to pay the war debt, Parliament decided, would be raised in part by levying taxes on the colonists. That in and of itself wasn't entirely unreasonable—after all, the military expenditures were made in defense of the colonists against the threat of the French and their Native cohorts. But it wouldn't be *what* as much as *how*. Americans, seeing themselves as equal partners in the cause of the empire, expected to have some say in the matter. Those conservatives in London who saw America as England's servant disagreed. To consult with colonial assemblies was to tacitly accept their legitimacy to a degree they were unwilling to allow.

America, in short, had to be shown its place.

Besides, there was no reason to believe that the provincial assemblies would agree on their own to being taxed, if past performances were anything to go by. Throughout the conflicts with France, when royal governors—the king or

The French claimed the land from the Great Lakes down behind the British colonies, effectively blocking off westward expansion.

queen's representative in the colony—asked respective provincial assemblies to raise funds, men or provisions for fortifications or expeditions against the French in Canada, they were often rebuked by claims that they were asking too much. The result was often bitter, career-ruining stalemate. Simply imposing a mandatory tax without bringing the quarrelsome provincial assemblies into things seemed best.

Nevertheless, the English government seems to have been unprepared for just how virulent the response would be when it decreed a tax on paper and paper products to take effect in 1766. It would be known as a "Stamp Act" or "Stamp Tax" owing to the stamps required on paper to show the tax

Above: A proof sheet showing the stamps required on paper to show the tax had been paid.

Left: Colonel Isaac Barre described the resistance to the Stamp Act in America as "sons of liberty." *Circa 1785, Gilbert Stuart, Brooklyn Museum.*

had been paid. British subjects had long been paying such taxes, so there was evidently no thought that Americans would do more than grumble. To their surprise and alarm, news of the tax was met with outright riots in Boston, Newport, New York and other colonial towns. Stamp agents who volunteered to collect the taxes were physically threatened and their homes torched. The very bureaucratic structure needed to enforce and realize revenue from the tax was falling apart under the strain.

Such violence wasn't entirely organic. It was egged on by secretive organizations formed to agitate for repeal, often by whatever means necessary.

Up to that point, the colonies had been sharply culturally individualistic—almost like independent nations unto themselves. But this threat brought them together in a way their own king or French predations on the frontiers had never before inspired. Not everyone in Parliament had been so tone-deaf to America, however. Colonel Isaac Barre, for example, saw the dangers in dismissing American angst, calling them "sons of liberty." As the individual resistance groups began seeing the advantages of working together, Barre's appellation stuck, and the whole network took to calling itself the Sons of Liberty.

The firestorm the Stamp Act unleashed—both in terms of violent but also nonviolent protestations like the "stamp act congress"—startled Parliament, but hardliners dug in their heels all the more. What really started shifting policymakers, however, was pressure from English manufacturers and merchants who suffered a loss of income as the pending tax damaged confidence in the colonial economy. With the whole situation spiraling out of control, Parliament repealed the Stamp Act on March 18, 1766, to the joy and celebration of the colonists. Few paid attention, however, to the accompanying Declaratory Act—a piece of legislation that proclaimed Parliament "had, hath, and of right ought to have, full power and authority to make laws and statutes of sufficient force and validity to bind the colonies and people of America...in all cases whatsoever."

In the broad sense, nothing had really changed. Parliament might repeal this one act as a face-saving expediency with one hand, but with the other it asserted its right to make other acts for America at will. Yet something *did* change. When that next time came, Americans had learned the lesson that sometimes even overt acts of civil disobedience get results.

The Townshend Acts

The economic problems caused by the costs of the war certainly didn't go away. Indeed, they would bedevil the administrations of three prime ministers, George Grenville (1763–65), the Second Marquess of Rockingham (1765–66) and the First Earl of Chatham (William Pitt the Elder; 1766–68). Lord Chatham's chancellor of the exchequer, however, thought he had the answer, albeit just more of the same. Charles Townshend concocted a new series of acts and regulations for America.

Together, the Revenue Act of 1767, the Indemnity Act, the Commissioners of Customs Act, the Vice Admiralty Court Act and the New York Restraining

Act are better known to history simply as the "Townshend Acts." They were designed to do a little more than just make America pay its tab. The funds raised would indeed go to England, but they would be reinvested in the colonies to pay the salaries of provincial governors and judges. Previously, these officials had relied on their respective colonies for their paychecks. By placing that responsibility on the English side of the Atlantic, it was felt these men would be less beholden to colonial influence and more ready to enforce trade regulations. It was, in effect, laying the groundwork for an even greater control over America. Thrown in for effect were punitive measures to restrain the powers of New York's provincial legislature until they agreed to comply with the Quartering Act, which they had rejected in 1765. The whole package was designed to keep America in its subservient place as a colony.

Resistance to the acts in America was just as virulent as over the Stamp Act, resting on a foundation of resentment laid by that previous tax. The American assertion was that Parliament should not have the right to inflict taxes on them unless they were represented in that body, just like any other loyal British subject.

The Sons of Liberty swung into action, too, along with others who shared in the resentment. Resistance came in three broad forms. At the one end were the politicians who earnestly believed that their grievances would be redressed by their good King George, if only they stuck to protesting through the established peaceful and respectful channels. The Massachusetts House of Representatives drafted a petition to the king and sent a letter to its fellow colonial assemblies encouraging them to do the same. As punishment, the Massachusetts Assembly was dissolved by its royal governor when it voted against rescinding the so-called Massachusetts Circular Letter.

A more middle tactic—and more effective—was the boycott. Parliament could easily ignore the petitions and fussing of people across an ocean who didn't vote for them. The same could decidedly not be said of their constituencies in England. When English manufacturers and merchants felt the pinch from the loss of American business during the Stamp Act crisis, they passed the pain on to their representatives. So began a concerted campaign across the colonies to boycott British imports until the Townshend Acts were also repealed.

The success of such a campaign, however, rested on the other end of the spectrum of resistance. It was more than some Americans could bear to wear crude homespun cloth, for example, instead of fine imported silks and ribbons of European fashion. Smugglers, who had long been part of the underground black markets that skirted regulations, found ready customers to buy their imports on the sly. Increasingly, however, they would find the Sons of Liberty standing between them and their clients. Non-importation pacts were created, and the names of merchants who signed on were hailed in the newspapers as true patriots worthy of public patronage. In addition to public shaming, those who failed to be so upstanding might find themselves paid a visit by unpleasant men. And woe unto anyone found buying imported goods as well. Disciplined unity behind the boycotts had to be maintained, even if it meant a little strong-arming.

The focus of the storm, however, would be Boston, where Parliament established a newly formed American Customs Board, tasked with enforcing the Townshend Acts. Not willing to risk another violent debacle as with the Stamp Act, regular British army troops were sent to occupy Boston and protect the board. This was different from the local militias Americans were used to, drawn from their own communities—this was, in effect, Great Britain occupying a major port city within its own colony as if it were that of an enemy nation.

The tensions created by the presence of these troops reached a critical mass on March 5, 1770, with what we now call the Boston Massacre, leaving five dead. The Sons of Liberty seized on the incident, using it as propaganda proving the malevolent intent of England to violate the liberties of its American subjects. Some in Parliament feared the whole thing was about to devolve into more bloodshed and perhaps even an open rebellion. As before, they would consent to repealing almost all of the taxes while at the same time making the face-saving reassertion that they reserved the prerogative to levy taxes at will.

But it was the one tax they chose to keep that would create an iconic protest that would reach directly into South Jersey.

The Boston Tea Party

Some Americans today lament the degree of power and influence wielded by modern corporations on government. Yet even the most egregiously influential tend to pale by comparison to the British East India Company. Imagine the most powerful multinational corporation you can think of. Now give it its very own private army and a charter to act in the role of a government in the foreign nations in which it does business.

That was how powerful the East India Company was.

Queen Elizabeth had granted it a royal charter in 1600, and while the government itself owned no stock, wealthy merchants and the aristocracy did, making the company a de facto spreader of the empire until its dissolution in 1874. It began trading primarily in cotton, silk, indigo dye, salt, saltpeter, tea and opium with the East Indies. But it was on the Indian subcontinent where it would really take root. After its private corporate army won the Battle of Plassey in 1757, the company became *the* government in India until 1858.

The East India Company had become adept at crushing local insurrections by 1770, but actual governing was no easy business. Profit was its overriding paramount concern, not without the occasionally deadly consequences. In the late 1760s, to cite one particularly ghastly example, the company raised land taxes on Bengali farmers by double, with another 10 percent hike in 1770. Impoverished farmers were then forced into growing more lucrative indigo and opium in place of food crops. The traditional laying in of reserves that had normally sustained them through periods of poor crop yield was outlawed as "hoarding." All of this conspired to make the people of Bengal especially vulnerable to the effects of a severe drought, resulting in a famine that wiped out a full third of the population.

Between this disaster and depressed trade in Europe, the company found itself in financial trouble. It looked to Parliament to help, and Parliament, in turn, looked to America. The Tea Tax of 1773 was designed to fix two problems. By giving the East India Company a monopoly over the tea imports into America through a waiving of the import duties imposed on competitors, the company would reap an expected windfall from the tax, helping to alleviate its financial distress. But it was also face-saving vindication—a reminder to those troublesome colonists in America that it was Parliament that still intended to call the shots.

The slogan "no taxation without representation" echoes in our culture as a demand for democracy. Yet this populist ideal was being used to advance the interests of a smaller group. Indeed, the average American had little cause to complain without it. In 1773, the average cost of legally imported tea actually *dropped*. Two specific groups would have a problem with that. One was the smugglers who found that the legal product was becoming cheaper than their illicit supply. But the ones who stood to really lose out were the *other* legal importers. The East India Company had not been the only dealer in tea, but now it enjoyed a government-supported near monopoly on the trade that threatened to force these other merchants out of the market. By placing anti-tax arguments within the context of taxation without representation, it was less about the economics of a few and more about the rights of the public as a whole.

It would seem that the government hadn't learned any lessons from the disaster of the Stamp Act. But those who had protested it had longer memories. Enforcement of the Tea Act, like the Stamp Act, required a bureaucracy on the American side of the equation. Instead of stamp agents tasked with accepting shipment of paper and collecting duties, now there were "consignees" tasked with accepting shipments of tea and collecting duties. The names and the commodities were different, but little else.

The American opposition, however, recalled that its most effective weapon had been the boycott. So a media campaign was mounted to encourage everyone to resist buying or dealing in East India Company tea. And the Sons of Liberty were there, ready to put the required pressures on those who failed to eschew such tea.

The results were effective. In October 1773, Philadelphians had forced a ship's captain to return to England with the tea still in its holds. Consignees resigned in Charleston, leaving the tea to be claimed by customs agents, and a ship on the way to New York, delayed by bad weather, found the consignees there had all resigned in the meantime. It, too, had to go home, having failed to deliver its cargo.

Indeed, it had gone well for the protestors pretty much everywhere—everywhere, that is, but Boston. The Massachusetts royal governor, Thomas Hutchinson, took a hardline against colonial recalcitrance and encouraged his consignees—including two of his sons—to stand firm. The showdown came with the arrival of the HMS *Dartmouth* and its cargo of tea in November 1773. The leader of the protestors in Boston, Samuel Adams, called for a mass meeting to decide what to do. To his delight, thousands of people showed up, forcing him to move the meeting from Faneuil Hall to the larger Old South Meeting House.

They knew that, by law, the *Dartmouth* had to be unloaded and the tax paid within twenty days of arrival at port. After that, it would be seized by customs. Adams and his followers issued resolutions urging Hutchinson to send the ship back to England without paying the duty. Given the governor's history, they knew this would be rebuked, so twenty-five men were sent to the dockside to keep watch over the *Dartmouth*, in case Hutchinson tried to offload the tea surreptitiously.

Needless to say, Hutchinson was not about to let the *Dartmouth* leave Boston Harbor still loaded. And in the meantime, two more ships had arrived, HMS *Eleanor* and HMS *Beaver* (a third, HMS *William* had been lost at sea to a storm). When the deadline for unloading the *Dartmouth* arrived on December 16, 1773, an estimated seven thousand people filled the Old South Meeting

The Boston
Tea Party as it
is imagined in
the American
creation myth.
"The Destruction
of Tea at Boston
Harbor," *1846,
Nathaniel Currier.*

House to receive word that Hutchinson remained unmoved. Adams tried to restrain the restless crowd, but they began heading for Griffin's Wharf, where the ships were moored.

This was the beginning of what we now call the Boston Tea Party, where some 342 chests of tea were seized by protestors and dumped overboard from the three ships over three hours. How active Adams had been in organizing things has been subject to debate—but he certainly grasped the publicity value immediately afterward. That there was indeed at least some forethought by someone is demonstrated by the often-noted fact that some of the mob dressed as Mohawk warriors. Aside from obviously helping obscure identities, there was a symbolism no one would have mistaken at the time. Like the coiled rattlesnake warning against being tread upon or the bald eagle, the Native American was a distinctly American thing—a symbolic assertion of an *American* identity in an act of civil disobedience.

At first, following the Revolution, it seems Americans were a little embarrassed by what amounted to vandalism and mob violence. And then, in the early 1830s, historians discovered that George Robert Twelves Hewes, one of the last surviving participants, was still around. Two biographies of him—along with the association of the event with Samuel Adams—helped to recast what had been a footnote into an iconic moment. As the early republic stood on its own, if sometimes shaky, legs, enough time had passed for a reassessment of the formative years as a historical narrative. What happened in Boston became known as a "tea party" for the first time in 1834, suggesting certain precocious nobility.

Other Tea Parties

What made the Boston protest unlike what had come before at Philadelphia and New York was the destruction of private property—the tea dumped into the harbor. Yet while it is the one most people know about, it was just one of three.

Word of what happened at Boston spread throughout the colonies. By spring, it had enflamed the revolutionary ire of the Sons of Liberty around the Maryland port of Chester Town (or Chestertown, as the place is known today). A meeting resulted in the so-called "Chester Town Resolves"—a list of grievances that included:

> *4ᵗʰ—RESOLVED, therefore, that whoever shall import, or in any way aid or assist in importing, or introducing from any part of Great Britain, or any other place whatsoever, into this town or country, any tea subject to the payment of a duty imposed by the aforesaid act of Parliament: or whoever shall willingly and knowingly sell, buy or consume, in any way assist with the sale, purchase or consumption of any tea imported as aforesaid subject to a duty, he or they, shall be stigmatized as enemies to the liberties of America.*

Shortly following their publication in the *Maryland Gazette*, word began to spread that a ship in the harbor, the brigantine HMS *Geddes*, had a consignment of tea in its hold. On May 23, 1774, a small group of men—in broad daylight and without native disguises, no less—were said to have forced their way onto the ship and tossed the tea into the Chester River.

Or did they?

Historians have since pointed out that while the resolves are a matter of historic record, there are no contemporary accounts of the destruction of the tea. Indeed, it does not appear to have been mentioned at all until 1899, leading some to conclude that it was an embellishment on the resolves in an effort to glom onto the fame of Boston.

There is no doubt, however, about the veracity of the Annapolis Tea Party of October 19, 1774, in Maryland. A brig, the *Peggy Stewart*, sailed into port with a cargo that included tea intended for local merchants Anthony Stewart and the brothers Joseph and James Williams. Stewart was part owner of the ship, which bore the name of his daughter. By then, the Annapolis branch of Sons of Liberty had begun pressuring merchants into joining the boycott, and the Williams brothers were nervous of attracting their wrath. Stewart, however, was more prepared to pay the tax, though he had a humanitarian excuse. Complicating matters was the presence of fifty-three indentured servants, who were also considered part of the cargo. According to the law, if the tea tax wasn't paid, none of the other cargo could be unloaded either, meaning those people were stuck in the middle, cramped in the ship until a compromise could be worked out. The *Peggy Stewart* was in need of an overhaul and had leaked on the voyage over. Sending it back to England, especially with the autumn storm season, Stewart reasoned, was as good as a death sentence to the passengers. He personally guaranteed that the tax would be paid, and the indentured servants at last disembarked. Part of the negotiation, however, had been that the tea would remain onboard until the Sons of Liberty could decide what to do with it.

Over the next five days came meetings that had as much to do with local politics as any quest for justice. Stewart and the Williams brothers met with committee chairman Charles Carroll, and a plan was made to burn the tea while publishing an apology in the *Maryland Gazette.* This wasn't enough for another committee member, however. Mathias Hammond published a handbill denouncing Stewart, desiring to make an example of the miscreants. Contemporary newspaper accounts conveniently left out mitigating details, such as the plight of the passengers or the fact that the Williams brothers had never been in favor of paying the tax. The result was a rising public thirst for punishment, even going so far as threatening Stewart with the gallows and the destruction of his home.

In the face of such vilification, Stewart offered a grand sacrificial gesture—he would personally put the *Peggy Stewart* to torch with the tea still in its hold. After reading a public apology, he, along with the Williams brothers, did just that on October 19, 1774. Within a few hours, it burned down to the waterline, and the public furor burned out with it. Anthony Stewart had saved his own skin. Not surprisingly, he was a Loyalist during the Revolution, living for a time in British-held New York before heading to Nova Scotia. With no small irony, he died in 1791 while traveling on business to, of all places, Annapolis.

Six days later, another "tea party" protest was organized in Edenton, North Carolina. What made this one remarkable wasn't any wonton destruction of private property—like Chestertown, it was a list of public resolves. This time, however, it was organized by women. Their gender may have been traditionally excluded from political and commercial life, but having the denizens of the domestic realm in line with the boycott of tea made obvious good sense. A gathering of fifty-one women, led by Penelope

Barker, met on October 25, 1774, vowing to give up tea and other British-made goods "until such time that all acts which tend to enslave our Native country shall be repealed."

"We are signing our names to a document, not hiding ourselves behind costumes like the men in Boston did at their tea party," the bold Ms. Barker wrote. "The British will know who we are." The one group the British hardliners were less apt to listen to besides the colonists was the colonists' women. But their misogynistic dismissal was shortsighted. Heralded as patriots, their example was held up for emulation by families throughout the colonies, only strengthening their cause.

The last of these "tea party" protests, however, would occur in December, down in South Jersey.

Greenwich Tea Party

At the end of 1774, the brig HMS *Greyhound* rounded the Capes of Delaware below New Jersey, intending on continuing up the Delaware River to land its consignment of tea at Philadelphia. Upon hearing of the inbound delivery, however, the citizens of the city convened and resolved that it would be no more permitted to offload its cargo than it would be at Boston or most other ports. A boatman brought the news to the *Greyhound*, no doubt to the annoyance of its Captain Allen.

If they couldn't land at a major port like Philadelphia, perhaps a more obscure town might be convinced to allow them in. Off Delaware Bay, up the Cohansey River, lay the village of Greenwich, New Jersey. The river was deep enough that it provided anchorage for ships approaching Philadelphia, making it a potential alternative. Best of all, it was home to Daniel Bowen, a loyalist Allen knew, who had no sympathy for the mobs who were interfering with the tea trade. Bowen would let the captain unload the tea into the cellar of his own home until it could be somehow brought into Philadelphia.

Bowen likely had no use for Philip Vickers Fithian. The twenty-seven-year-old Presbyterian minister trainee was decidedly on the opposite side of the questions of the day from Bowen. He had passed through Annapolis on his way home to New Jersey shortly after the tea burning there and was likely inspired by the example when it came to his hometown's response to the tea in Bowen's cellar.

The home of Daniel Bowen as it is today, a private residence. *Courtesy of the author.*

Needless to say, those in town who supported the boycott were not happy with Bowen's decision. A group of them had gathered at the home of Richard Howell to decide what to do on December 22. They left and rode the four miles to Fithian's home, from which they later emerged, dressed as Native Americans. Breaking into Bowen's cellar, they dragged the tea out and off into a distant field to set it on fire.

The merchants expecting their tea were obviously upset, appealing to New Jersey's royal governor, William Franklin, for action. Disguises aside, there was little doubt who the men were in so small a community. So Franklin sent Sheriff Jonathan Elmer to go and arrest them. Elmer did his duty, even taking in his own relatives. There would be no hard feelings, however, since they all knew that the case against them was already lost to what we today would call jury nullification. This had long been the bane of the Crown's legal interests in the colonies. Juries were picked by the sheriff and, given the tightknit communities, often ended up including friends and relatives of the accused. Among the jurists at the trial of the tea burners, for example, was Daniel Elmer, the sheriff's own nephew.

If someone was truly guilty of a crime, he would be punished, of course, regardless. But in this instance, when most of the town was sympathetic to the cause of the accused, it was really all just for show. As expected, they returned a finding of "no cause for action." This was an affront to the governor, who had Sheriff Elmer removed from office. In a stunning example of conflict of interest, he appointed in his place none other than Daniel Bowen! Nevertheless, he was no match for a jury that had already made up its mind, and a second court found the same result. Seeing the futility, the case was dropped.

In the coming year, as violent revolution began, they would all have a lot more to worry about than burnt tea.

Many of the men involved in the Greenwich Tea Party would go on to play important roles in the coming war. Shortly following his marriage to Elizabeth Beatty on October 25, 1775, Philip Vickers Fithian shipped off as a chaplain in the New Jersey Militia, witnessing the Battle of Long Island and Battle of Harlem Heights before dying near Fort Washington on October 8, 1776, at the age of twenty-nine. Three others from that night would also die in the war.

Richard Howell, in whose home they first met, would go on to be elected governor of New Jersey in 1792 and was succeeded by Joseph Bloomfield, who had defended the accused at their two show trials.

Daniel Bowen remained loyal to the king, joining the British army as a captain when it occupied Philadelphia. Like many Loyalists, he never returned to New Jersey, settling after the war in Nova Scotia.

Cumberland Boys

Depending on which side of the argument one sat, the "tea parties" were either the criminal destruction of property or justified acts of civil disobedience. As the Boston Tea Party was rediscovered and reconsidered in the 1830s, the towns where the other "parties" took place wanted their share of recognition, too.

"It is well known that the 'Boston Boys' boast not a little of their ancestors having thrown overboard the tea in Boston Harbor," New York's *Rondout Freeman* newspaper reported in its April 25, 1846 edition, "but it is not generally known that a like occurrence took place in the state of New-Jersey of which 'Cumberland Boys' also boast."

The Tea Burner Monument. *Courtesy of the author.*

Taking pride in their ancestors' roles, memorializing the Greenwich tea burning became the centerpiece around which the Cumberland County Historical Society was founded. At 2:00 p.m. on December 2, 1908, a group of local historians met at the old Cumberland County Courthouse to discuss plans for erecting a monument to the event. They intended on soliciting funds from the Board of Freeholders and state legislators and needed a nonprofit entity to handle the money. But the long-term goal was to establish a county historical society that would continue on after the project was done.

O.J. Hammell Company, Inc., from Absecon, New Jersey, was hired for the job, having had a good reputation creating many of the Civil War monuments gracing town squares along the East Coast, as well as private grave markers. The Tea Burner Monument still stands in a pleasant small park on the corner of Market Street and Ye Greate Street. Along these sleepy streets may be found many examples of homes dating back to the eighteenth century—silent witnesses to when South Jersey played a role in events that changed the world.

Sources

Chapter 1

Everhart, Mike. "The Cope-Marsh Feud." *New York Heralds.* http://www. oceansofkansas.com/NYHerald.html.Gallagher, William B. *When Dinosaurs Roamed New Jersey.* N.p.: self-published, 1997. Reprint, 2003.

Laurie, Maxine N., Peter O. Wacker and Michael Siegel. *Mapping New Jersey: An Evolving Landscape.* New Brunswick, NJ: Rivergate Books, 2009.

Lesley, J.P. "Obituary Notice of Wm. Parker Foulke." *Proceedings of the American Philosophical Society* 10 (January 1865–December 1868): 481–92.

Mazzetta, Gerardo V., Per Christiansen and Richard A. Farin. "Giants and Bizarres: Body Size of Some Southern South American Cretaceous Dinosaurs." *Historical Biology* (2004): 1–13.

New York Herald. "The Savans of 1870." August 19, 1870.

New York Times. "New Jersey Marl: Opening of a Rich Bed in Monmouth County—A New and Cheap Fertilizer—Increased Facilities for Exportation." July 2, 1869. www.nytimes.com (accessed October 23, 2012).

Proceedings of the Academy of Natural Sciences of Philadelphia. Minutes of December 14th meeting, 1858.

Chapter 2

"Auto Theater Has 460 Loudspeakers." *Popular Science* (October 1935): 32.
"Drive-In Movie Holds Four Hundred Cars." *Popular Mechanics* (September 1933): 326.
Segrave, Kerry. *Drive-in Theaters: A History from Their Inception in 1933.* N.p.: McFarland & Company, Inc., 2006.

Chapter 3

Barnes, Harry E. *A History of the Penal, Reformatory and Correctional Institutions of the State of New Jersey: Analytical and Documentary.* New York: Arno Press, 1918.
Death Penalty USA. "U.S.A. Executions, 1607–1976." http://deathpenaltyusa.org/usa1/state/new_jersey1.htm

Chapter 4

Dawson, Jim. *Rock Around the Clock: The Record That Started the Rock Revolution!* San Francisco: Backbeat Books, 2005.
Dawson, Jim, and Steve Propes. *What Was the First Rock 'n' Roll Record?* London: Faber and Faber, 1992.
PR Web. "Birthplace of Rock and Roll—Wildwood, New Jersey, Stakes Its Claim." http://www.prweb.com/releases/2004/04/prweb117635.htm.

Chapter 5

Blanchard, Jean-Pierre. "Journal of My Forty-Fifth Ascension Being the First Performed in America." *Magazine of History with Notes and Queries* 64 (1914).
Roncase, Kelly. "John-Pierre Blanchard's Balloon Landing, a Major Part of Deptford's History, Turns 217." *South Jersey Times,* January 5, 2010.
Wood, James. *The Nuttall Encyclopedia.* New York: Frederick Warne, 1907.

Chapter 6

Bradford, Sarah. *Harriet Tubman, The Moses of Her People*. Bedford, MA: Applewood Books, 1869. Reprint, 1993.

Clinton, Catherine. *Harriet Tubman: The Road to Freedom*. Lulu.com, 2004.

Humez, Jean M. *Harriet Tubman: The Life and the Life Stories*. Madison: University of Wisconsin Press, 2006.

Siebert, Wilbur Henry. *The Underground Railroad from Slavery to Freedom*. London: Macmillan Company, 1898.

Switala, William J. *Underground Railroad: In Delaware, Maryland and West Virginia*. Mechanicsburg, PA: Stackpole Books, 2004.

Chapter 7

Cumberland County Historical Society. http://www.cchistsoc.org/teaburnerscelebration.html.

Get NJ. "Stories of New Jersey." http://www.getnj.com/storiesofnewjersey/sojpg93.shtml.

"History of the O.J. Hammell Co." http://www.ojhammell.com.

Skirbst, Henry F. *Tales of A Battleground: New Jersey's Role in the Era of the American Revolution*. N.p.: AuthorHouse, 2006.

ABOUT THE AUTHOR

G ordon Bond is an independent historian, author and lecturer. He is
the founder and editor-in-chief of Garden State Legacy, a free online
quarterly magazine of New Jersey history (www.GardenStateLegacy.com).
He is the author of "James Parker: A Printer on the Eve of Revolution"
(*Garden State Legacy*, 2010), *North Jersey Legacies: Hidden History from the Gateway
to the Skylands* (The History Press, 2012) and *Treasured Artifacts of the Garden
State* (The History Press, Fall 2013). He has also written a history of the 1951
Woodbridge, New Jersey train wreck and is presently researching a book
about Thomas Mundy Peterson, the first African American to vote under
the Fifteenth Amendment to the U.S. Constitution. He lives in Union, New
Jersey, with his wife, architectural conservator Stephanie M. Hoagland, and
their two cats, Onslow and Daisy. Gordon and Stephanie have been jointly
studying New Jersey's folk grave marker traditions.

Visit us at
www.historypress.net
....
This title is also available as an e-book